GREAT CHRISTIAN CLASSICS

FOUR ESSENTIAL WORKS OF THE FAITH

Student Workbook

Edited by Kevin Swanson
and Joshua Schwisow

Generations

Copyright © 2020 by Generations

ISBN: 978-1-7350719-3-0

1st Printing, 2020.

All rights reserved.
Printed in the United States of America

Published by:
Generations
PO Box 1398
Elizabeth, CO 80107-1398
www.generations.org

For more information on this and
other titles from Generations,
visit www.generations.org

Table of Contents

Using This Student Workbook 4
Course Description 5
Suggested Daily Schedule 7
Worksheets 15
Worksheet Answer Key 325
Essay Grading Criteria 360

Using This Student Workbook

Features: The suggested weekly schedule enclosed has easy-to-manage lessons that guide the reading, worksheets, and all assessments. The pages of this guide are perforated and three-hole punched, so materials are easy to tear out, hand out, grade, and store. Teachers are encouraged to adjust the schedule and materials needed in order to best work within their unique educational program.

Lesson Scheduling: Students are instructed to read the pages in their book and then complete the corresponding section provided by the teacher. Usually, students will read and complete a worksheet on the same day, but occasionally the readings and worksheets may be scheduled for separate days, due to length. Assessments that may include worksheets, essays, and examinations are provided, with space to record each grade. Space is provided on the weekly schedule for assignment dates, and flexibility in scheduling is encouraged. Teachers may adapt the scheduled days per each unique student situation. As the student completes each assignment, this can be marked with an "X" in the box.

Course Description

In this exploration of *Great Christian Classics: Four Essential Works of the Faith*, the student will complete coursework for the following books:

- ✓ *On the Incarnation* by Athanasius
- ✓ *The Imitation of Christ* by Thomas A'Kempis
- ✓ *The Institutes of the Christian Religion* (abridged) by John Calvin
- ✓ *The Pilgrim's Progress* by John Bunyan

Grading Options for This Course

It is always the prerogative of an educator to assess student grades however he or she might deem best. The following is only a suggested guideline based on the material presented through this course:

To calculate the percentage of the worksheets and quizzes the educator may use the following guide. Divide total number of correct questions (example: 43) by the total number of questions possible (example: 46) to calculate the percentage out of 100 possible. 43/46 = 93 percent correct.

The suggested grade values are noted as follows: 90 to 100 percent = A; 80 to 89 percent = B; 70 to 79 percent = C; 60 to 69 percent = D; and 0 to 59 percent = F.

Vocabulary

Vocabulary exercises are found throughout the workbook. These exercises are divided between matching exercises and sentence construction. For help finding definitions, the student should consult a print or online English dictionary. The textbook also contains many definitions in the explanatory notes to aid the student.

Essays

There are four essay assignments for each of the works contained in the textbook. Essay Grading Criteria is provided at the end of this student workbook.

Exams

There are four exams for each of the works contained in the textbook. These exams should be completed by the student without consulting the textbook.

First Semester Suggested Daily Schedule

Date	Day	Assignment	Due Date	✓	Grade
		First Semester-First Quarter			
Week 1	Day 1	**ON THE INCARNATION - ATHANASIUS** Read Introduction			
	Day 2				
	Day 3	Read Chapter 1: Creation and the Fall and Complete Assignments			
	Day 4				
	Day 5				
Week 2	Day 6	Read Ch. 2: The Divine Dilemma and Its Solution in the Incarnation (Pt 1) & Complete Assignments			
	Day 7				
	Day 8	Read Ch. 3: The Divine Dilemma and Its Solution in the Incarnation (Pt 2) & Complete Assignments			
	Day 9				
	Day 10				
Week 3	Day 11	Read Chapter 4: The Death of Christ and Complete Assignments			
	Day 12				
	Day 13	Read Chapter 5: The Resurrection and Complete Assignments			
	Day 14				
	Day 15				
Week 4	Day 16	Read Chapter 6: Refutation of the Jews and Complete Assignments			
	Day 17				
	Day 18	Read Chapter 7: Refutation of the Gentiles (Part 1) and Complete Assignments			
	Day 19				
	Day 20				
Week 5	Day 21	Read Chapter 8: Refutation of the Gentiles (Part II) and Complete Assignments			
	Day 22				
	Day 23	Read Chapter 9: Conclusion and Complete Assignments			
	Day 24				
	Day 25				
Week 6	Day 26	Complete Essay Assignment			
	Day 27				
	Day 28	Complete Exam			
	Day 29				
	Day 30				

Great Christian Classics: Four Essential Works of the Faith 7

Date	Day	Assignment	Due Date	✓	Grade
Week 7	Day 31	**THE IMITATION OF CHRIST – THOMAS A'KEMPIS** Read Introduction			
	Day 32				
	Day 33	Read Book 1: Sections 1-5 and Complete Assignments			
	Day 34				
	Day 35	Read Book 1: Sections 6-10 and Complete Assignments			
Week 8	Day 36	Read Book 1: Sections 11-14 and Complete Assignments			
	Day 37				
	Day 38	Read Book 1: Sections 15-17 and Complete Assignments			
	Day 39				
	Day 40	Read Book 1: Sections 18-20 and Complete Assignments			
Week 9	Day 41	Read Book 1: Sections 21-23 and Complete Assignments			
	Day 42				
	Day 43	Read Book 1: Sections 24-25 and Complete Assignments			
	Day 44				
	Day 45	Read Book 2: Sections 1-5 and Complete Assignments			
		First Semester-Second Quarter			
Week 1	Day 46	Read Book 2: Sections 6-8 and Complete Assignments			
	Day 47				
	Day 48	Read Book 2: Sections 9-12 and Complete Assignments			
	Day 49				
	Day 50	Read Book 3: Section 1-2 and Complete Assignments			
Week 2	Day 51	Read Book 3: Sections 3-6 and Complete Assignments			
	Day 52				
	Day 53	Read Book 3: Sections 7-10 and Complete Assignments			
	Day 54				
	Day 55	Read Book 3: Sections 11-14 and Complete Assignments			
Week 3	Day 56	Read Book 3: Sections 15-17 and Complete Assignments			
	Day 57				
	Day 58	Read Book 3: Sections 18-20 and Complete Assignments			
	Day 59				
	Day 60	Read Book 3: Sections 21-24 and Complete Assignments			

Date	Day	Assignment	Due Date	✓	Grade
Week 4	Day 61	Read Book 3: Sections 25-27 and Complete Assignments			
	Day 62				
	Day 63	Read Book 3: Sections 28-30 and Complete Assignments			
	Day 64				
	Day 65	Read Book 3: Sections 31-33 and Complete Assignments			
Week 5	Day 66	Read Book 3: Sections 34-37 and Complete Assignments			
	Day 67				
	Day 68	Read Book 3: Sections 38-40 and Complete Assignments			
	Day 69				
	Day 70	Read Book 3: Sections 41-44 and Complete Assignments			
Week 6	Day 71	Read Book 3: Sections 45-47 and Complete Assignments			
	Day 72				
	Day 73	Read Book 3: Sections 48-52 and Complete Assignments			
	Day 74				
	Day 75	Read Book 3: Sections 53-59 and Complete Assignments			
Week 7	Day 76	Read Book 4: Sections 1-5 and Complete Assignments			
	Day 77				
	Day 78	Read Book 4: Sections 6-10 and Complete Assignments			
	Day 79				
	Day 80	Read Book 4: Sections 11-15 and Complete Assignments			
Week 8	Day 81	Read Book 4: Sections 16-18 and Complete Assignments			
	Day 82				
	Day 83	Complete Essay Assignment			
	Day 84				
	Day 85				
Week 9	Day 86				
	Day 87				
	Day 88	Complete Exam			
	Day 89				
	Day 90				
		Mid-Term Grade			

Second Semester Suggested Daily Schedule

Date	Day	Assignment	Due Date	✓	Grade
		Second Semester–Third Quarter			
Week 1	Day 91	**INSTITUTES OF THE CHRISTIAN RELIGION – JOHN CALVIN** Read Book 1: Ch. 1-2 and Complete Assignments			
	Day 92				
	Day 93	Read Book 1: Chapters 3-4 and Complete Assignments			
	Day 94				
	Day 95	Read Book 1: Chapters 5-6 and Complete Assignments			
Week 2	Day 96	Read Book 1: Chapter 7, 9, 13 and Complete Assignments			
	Day 97				
	Day 98	Read Book 1: Chapters 14-15 and Complete Assignments			
	Day 99				
	Day 100	Read Book 1: Chapters 16-17 and Complete Assignments			
Week 3	Day 101	Read Book 2: Chapters 1-3 and Complete Assignments			
	Day 102				
	Day 103	Read Book 2: Chapters 6-8 and Complete Assignments			
	Day 104				
	Day 105	Read Book 2: Chapter 9 and Complete Assignments			
Week 4	Day 106	Read Book 2: Chapter 12, 14 and Complete Assignments			
	Day 107				
	Day 108	Read Book 2: Chapter 15-16 and Complete Assignments			
	Day 109				
	Day 110	Read Book 3: Chapters 1-3 and Complete Assignment			
Week 5	Day 111	Read Book 3: Chapters 6-8 and Complete Assignments			
	Day 112				
	Day 113	Read Book 3: Chapters 9-10 and Complete Assignments			
	Day 114				
	Day 115	Read Book 3: Chapters 11-12 and Complete Assignments			

Date	Day	Assignment	Due Date	✓	Grade
Week 6	Day 116	Read Book 3: Chapters 13-14 and Complete Assignments			
	Day 117				
	Day 118	Read Book 3: Chapters 16-17 and Complete Assignments			
	Day 119				
	Day 120	Read Book 3: Chapters 19-21 and Complete Assignments			
Week 7	Day 121	Read Book 3: Chapter 22, 24, 25 and Complete Assignments			
	Day 122				
	Day 123	Read Book 4: Chapters 1-3 and Complete Assignments			
	Day 124				
	Day 125	Read Book 4: Chapter 12, 14 and Complete Assignments			
Week 8	Day 126	Read Book 4: Chapters 15-17 and Complete Assignments			
	Day 127				
	Day 128	Complete Essay Assignment			
	Day 129				
	Day 130				
Week 9	Day 131				
	Day 132				
	Day 133	Complete Exam			
	Day 134				
	Day 135				
		Second Semester-Fourth Quarter			
Week 1	Day 136	**THE PILGRIM'S PROGRESS – JOHN BUNYAN** Read Introduction			
	Day 137				
	Day 138	Read The Author's Apology for His Book			
	Day 139				
	Day 140	Read Book 1: Chapter 1 and Complete Assignments			

Date	Day	Assignment	Due Date	✓	Grade
	Day 141	Read Book 1: Chapter 2 and Complete Assignments			
	Day 142				
Week 2	Day 143	Read Book 1: Chapter 3 and Complete Assignments			
	Day 144				
	Day 145				
	Day 146	Read Book 1: Chapter 4 and Complete Assignments			
	Day 147				
Week 3	Day 148	Read Book 1: Chapter 5 and Complete Assignments			
	Day 149				
	Day 150				
	Day 151	Read Book 1: Chapter 6 and Complete Assignments			
	Day 152				
Week 4	Day 153	Read Book 1: Chapter 7 and Complete Assignments			
	Day 154				
	Day 155				
	Day 156	Read Book 1: Chapter 8 and Complete Assignments			
	Day 157				
Week 5	Day 158	Read Book 1: Chapter 9 and Complete Assignments			
	Day 159				
	Day 160	Read Book 1: Chapter 10 and Complete Assignments			
	Day 161	Read Book 2: The Author's Way			
	Day 162				
Week 6	Day 163	Read Book 2: To the Reader and Complete Assignments			
	Day 164				
	Day 165	Read Book 2: Chapter 1 and Complete Assignments			

Date	Day	Assignment	Due Date	✓	Grade
Week 7	Day 166	Read Book 2: Chapter 2 and Complete Assignments			
	Day 167				
	Day 168	Read Book 2: Chapter 3 and Complete Assignments			
	Day 169				
	Day 170	Read Book 2: Chapter 4 and Complete Assignments			
Week 8	Day 171	Read Book 2: Chapter 5 and Complete Assignments			
	Day 172				
	Day 173	Read Book 2: Chapter 6 and Complete Assignments			
	Day 174				
	Day 175	Read Book 2: Chapter 7 and Complete Assignments			
Week 9	Day 176	Read Book 2: Chapter 8 and Complete Assignments			
	Day 177				
	Day 178	Complete Essay Assignment			
	Day 179				
	Day 180	Complete Exam			
		Final Grade			

On the Incarnation — Chapter 1 Worksheet 1 — Name

VOCABULARY 1. Match the word with the correct definition

1. Traduce

2. Wiseacres

3. Impute

4. Artificer

a. to expose to shame or blame by means of falsehood and misrepresentation.

b. a person who possesses or affects to possess great wisdom.

c. a skillful or artistic worker; craftsperson

d. to attribute or describe

VOCABULARY 2. Use each word in a sentence of your own construction.

1. Traduce –
   Your Sentence:

2. Wiseacres –
   Your Sentence:

3. Impute –
   Your Sentence:

4. Artificer –
   Your Sentence:

On the Incarnation | Chapter 1 Worksheet 2 | Name

Study Questions

1. What subject(s) did the previous book ("Against the Gentiles") cover?

2. Who is Athanasius addressing in this book? Is he a believer?

3. What do the Jews and Greeks think about the doctrine of Christ being both God and man?

4. How does the Christian faith stand against the derision of unbelievers? What is its greatest apologetic?

5. Why did Christ assume a human body? What does Athanasius present as the "sole reason"?

6. Christ is the agent of two different works. What are they?

7. What do the Epicureans teach about the origination of the universe?

8. How does Athanasius argue against the Epicureans?

9. What do the Platonists teach about the origination of the universe?

10. How does Athanasius argue against the Platonists?

11. What do the Gnostics teach about the origination of the universe?

12. How does Athanasius argue against the Gnostics?

13. How did man differ from the animals in God's creation?

14. What happened to man when he disobeyed God in the garden?

15. What is man's nature, in Athanasius' words?

16. What is evil?

17. What are the worst sins committed by men, as listed by Athanasius?

18. From what books of the Bible (and apocryphal books) does Athanasius quote?

On the Incarnation | Chapter 2 Worksheet 1 | Name

VOCABULARY 1. Match the word with the correct definition

1. Incorporeal
2. Wiseacres
3. Liability
4. Untainted
5. Appropriation
6. Incurred

a. to become liable or subject to through one's own action

b. not corporeal or material; insubstantial

c. no trace of infection, contamination, or the like

d. setting apart, authorizing, or legislating for some specific purpose or use

e. debts or pecuniary obligations

f. a person who possesses or affects to possess great wisdom.

VOCABULARY 2. Use each word in a sentence of your own construction.

1. Incorporeal –
   Your Sentence:

2. Incorruptible –
   Your Sentence:

3. Liability –
   Your Sentence:

4. Untainted –
   Your Sentence:

5. Appropriation –
   Your Sentence:

6. Incurred –
   Your Sentence:

On the Incarnation — Chapter 2, Worksheet 2 — Name

STUDY QUESTIONS

1. Why was God bound to keep man in a condition of death?

2. Why was it so "monstrous and unfitting" that man should remain in this state of death?

3. Why couldn't man save himself by repenting?

4. What three things was Jesus qualified to do in order to save mankind?

5. What is the only way that man's corruption could be addressed? How does this relate to the Son of God becoming man?

6. What analogy does Athanasius give for our association with Christ in His life-giving capacity?

7. What two things did Jesus do for us at the cross?

On the Incarnation | Chapter 3 Worksheet 1 | Name

VOCABULARY 1. Match the word with the correct definition

1. Impiety

2. Immolated

3. Colonize

4. Obliterate

5. Paradox

6. Faculty (Ability)

a. to form a colony

b. a statement or proposition that seems self-contradictory or absurd but in reality expresses a possible truth

c. to remove or destroy all traces of; do away with; destroy completely

d. lack of piety; lack of reverence for God or sacred things; irreverence

e. an ability, natural or acquired, for a particular kind of action

f. to destroy by fire

VOCABULARY 2. Use each word in a sentence of your own construction

1. Impiety –
   Your Sentence:

2. Immolated –
   Your Sentence:

3. Colonize –
   Your Sentence:

4. Obliterate –
   Your Sentence:

Great Christian Classics: Four Essential Works of the Faith   25

5. Paradox –
   Your Sentence:

6. Faculty (Ability) –
   Your Sentence:

On the Incarnation — Chapter 3, Worksheet 2 — Name

Study Questions

1. What makes man different from the animals, according to Athanasius?

2. How does Athanasius distinguish human beings (created in the image of God) from Christ, the Son of God?

3. How does Athanasius describe the depravity of man in this section?

4. What are the 3-4 ways in which God revealed the truth to sinful men?

5. Why did man willfully continue in deceitfulness?

6. Why was it impossible for angels to solve the problem of man's corruption?

7. What illustration does Athanasius use to show what has happened to the image of God in man?

8. Why were fallen men incapable of presenting an accurate message concerning God?

9. Why is natural revelation (creation) now insufficient to teach men about the Father and about sin?

10. What kind of a teacher is Christ?

11. How did Christ oppose error or false thinking?

12. What is the great paradox of the incarnation?

13. What does God do? What does the Word do in relation to the universe continually?

14. How do we know that Jesus was truly man?

15. How did Christ prove His divinity while He was on earth?

On the Incarnation — Chapter 4 Worksheet 1 — Name

VOCABULARY 1. Match the word with the correct definition

1. Primal
2. Banished
3. Dissolution
4. Consonant
5. Annulled
6. Antagonists

a. a person who is opposed to, struggles against, or competes with another; opponent; adversary
b. first; original; primeval
c. to make void or null; abolish; cancel
d. the act or process of resolving or dissolving into parts or elements
e. in agreement; agreeable; in accord; consistent
f. to compel to depart; send, drive, or put away

VOCABULARY 2. Use each word in a sentence of your own construction.

1. Primal –
   Your Sentence:

2. Banished –
   Your Sentence:

3. Dissolution –
   Your Sentence:

4. Consonant –
   Your Sentence:

5. Annulled –
   Your Sentence:

6. Antagonists –
   Your Sentence:

On the Incarnation — Chapter 4, Worksheet 2 — Name

STUDY QUESTIONS

1. How did creation confess to Christ's victory at the cross?

2. How does Athanasius know that this really happened?

3. What is the very center of our faith?

4. For whom did Jesus die?

5. What does Athanasius say about the body of Christ?

6. Why did Jesus have to die by crucifixion, according to Athanasius?

7. What is the marvelous and mighty paradox in Christ's death?

8. What is the biblical reason for the death on the cross?

9. What symbolism does Athanasius find in Christ being "lifted up?"

On the Incarnation | Chapter 5 Worksheet 1 | Name

VOCABULARY 1. Match the word with the correct definition

1. Impassable
2. Deriders
3. Vanquished
4. Bereft
5. Ostentation
6. Pursuance
7. Irrefragable

a. Those who laugh in scorn or contempt; scoff or jeer at; mock
b. pretentious or conspicuous show, as of wealth or importance; display intended to impress others
c. the following or carrying out of some plan, course, injunction, or the like
d. unable to be surmounted
e. not to be disputed or contested
f. to conquer or subdue by superior force, as in battle
g. deprived; parted from

VOCABULARY 2. Use each word in a sentence of your own construction

1. Impassable –
   Your Sentence:

2. Deriders –
   Your Sentence:

3. Vanquished –
   Your Sentence:

4. Bereft –

Your Sentence:

5. Ostentation –
Your Sentence:

6. Pursuance –
Your Sentence:

7. Irrefragable –
Your Sentence:

On the Incarnation — Chapter 5, Worksheet 2 — Name

STUDY QUESTIONS

1. Why did Jesus wait three days before the resurrection?

2. What effect did the resurrection of Christ have on His followers?

3. What do women think of death?

4. What do young boys and girls think about death?

5. How do we wrap ourselves in asbestos and enter the fire, in the spiritual sense?

6. How is death overcome in the life of the Christian (two things)?

7. **Research Question**: What is the sign of the cross to which Athanasius keeps referring? Is it legitimate?

8. What does Athanasius think about the present state of the lion or the snake? What do these represent? Use Scripture references.

9. What exactly was it that brought about the destruction of death?

10. How does Christ prove His resurrection in His followers?

11. What should Christians call dead?

12. How do we learn about the invisible God?

13. Why do men deny the truth of the resurrection when it is so obvious? Is the truth as obvious today as it was then?

On the Incarnation | Chapter 6 Worksheet 1 | Name

VOCABULARY 1. Match the word with the correct definition

1. Incongruity   a. not to be appeased, mollified, or pacified

2. Surmises   b. out of keeping or place; inappropriate; unbecoming

3. Despoiling   c. shameless or impudent

4. Implacable   d. a conjecture or opinion

5. Brazenly   e. to strip of possessions, things of value, etc.; rob; plunder; pillage

6. Demented   f. crazy; insane; mad

VOCABULARY 2. Use each word in a sentence of your own construction

1. Incongruity –
   Your Sentence:

2. Surmises –
   Your Sentence:

3. Despoiling –
   Your Sentence:

4. Implacable –
   Your Sentence:

Great Christian Classics: Four Essential Works of the Faith   39

5. Brazenly –
   Your Sentence:

6. Demented –
   Your Sentence:

| *On the Incarnation* | Chapter 6 Worksheet 2 | Name |

Study Questions

1. How does Athanasius argue his case for Christ's incarnation and death here?

2. What Old Testament verses does he use to defend Christ's taking on human flesh?

3. What Old Testament chapter does he refer to in order to defend Christ's death?

4. What are the singularly remarkable elements of Christ's birth (compared to other biblical figures)?

5. What did Christ the King do in Egypt that Moses and Abraham did not do? When did this happen?

6. What Old Testament Bible verses does Athanasius use to describe the manner of Christ's death?

7. How does Christ appear superior to David, Moses, and the prophets?

8. How do we know that Isaiah 35:3-6 was fulfilled at the time of Christ?

9. Why is Daniel 9:24, 25 so convincing a proof for Athanasius?

10. When did Kings, Prophets, and Visions stop for the Old Testament Jews?

11. What has happened to heathen idolatry over the last 2000 years in places like Italy, Greece, Egypt, etc.?

12. How does Athanasius express his optimism concerning Christ's presence in the world? Quote him. Is the Christian church in America (or in your experience) this optimistic? How does this underscore the faith of this author?

On the Incarnation — Chapter 7, Worksheet 1 — Name

VOCABULARY 1. Match the word with the correct definition

1. Confute
2. Actuate
3. Pervades
4. Vitiate
5. Intrinsic
6. Endued
7. Thrall

a. to invest or endow with some gift, quality, or faculty
b. to prove (a person) to be wrong by argument or proof
c. to impair the quality of; make faulty; spoil
d. to incite or move to action; impel; motivate
e. a person who is in bondage; slave
f. belonging to a thing by its very nature
g. to become spread throughout all parts of

VOCABULARY 2. Use each word in a sentence of your own construction

1. Confute –
   Your Sentence:

2. Actuate –
   Your Sentence:

3. Pervades –
   Your Sentence:

4. Vitiate –
   Your Sentence:

5. Intrinsic –
   Your Sentence:

6. Endued –
   Your Sentence:

7. Thrall –
   Your Sentence:

On the Incarnation | Chapter 7 Worksheet 2 | Name

Study Questions

1. What apologetic method does Athanasius choose to use in the first paragraph?

2. How does Athanasius argue the reasonableness of the Word taking on a human body?

3. How does Athanasius use the example of the human mind controlling the body?

4. Why did Jesus choose to come as a human rather than into the sun or moon?

5. How does Athanasius argue from Plato's perspective?

6. Why couldn't God have re-created (saved) mankind by a command, in the same sort of way that He created the world?

7. How does Jesus manifest His Lordship and deity among men?

On the Incarnation — Chapter 8, Worksheet 1 — Name

VOCABULARY 1. Match the word with the correct definition

1. Spurn
2. Attest
3. Chastity
4. Imposture
5. Sophists
6. Compunction
7. Disrepute
8. Transcend
9. Epiphany

a. a person who reasons adroitly and speciously rather than soundly
b. undefiled or stainless
c. bad repute; low regard; disfavor
d. an appearance or manifestation, especially of a deity
e. any uneasiness or hesitation about the rightness of an action
f. the action or practice of imposing fraudulently upon others
g. to reject with disdain; scorn
h. to bear witness to; certify; declare to be correct, true, or genuine
i. to rise above or go beyond; overpass; exceed

VOCABULARY 2. Use each word in a sentence of your own construction

1. Spurn –
   Your Sentence:

2. Attest –
   Your Sentence:

3. Chastity –
   Your Sentence:

4. Imposture –
   Your Sentence:

5. Sophists –
   Your Sentence:

6. Compunction –
   Your Sentence:

7. Disrepute –
   Your Sentence:

8. Transcend –
   Your Sentence:

9. Epiphany –
   Your Sentence:

On the Incarnation | Chapter 8 Worksheet 2 | Name

STUDY QUESTIONS

1. What has happened in the Roman Empire up to AD 310 that would indicate Christ the Word really came to earth?

2. Where were the centers of the "oracles" or pagan prophets?

3. What were the nations that used magic to fill people with wonder and fear?

4. How does Athanasius refer to classical Greek philosophy? What has happened to it?

5. How does Christ compare to Greek philosophy?

6. Who does Athanasius point to as the greatest exemplars of the Christian faith?

7. How are the demons routed and witchcraft confounded? Comment.

8. How does Athanasius address the charge that Christ is a magician?

9. How does Athanasius address the charge that Christ is a demon? How did Christ address this charge himself?

10. How does Christ compare to the Greek healer, Aesculapius?

11. How does Christ compare with the Greek god Dionysus?

12. How did Christ compare to the Greek philosophers (while they lived)?

13. What did Christ do to the barbarian and heathen folk?

14. What did the Greeks teach about resurrection?

15. How far had the Gospel penetrated at the point of Athanasius' writings?

16. What was travel like in these pagan lands before Christ showed up?

17. Which Scripture was fulfilled among many of these pagan lands?

18. How do we engage the real conflict? How do we fight the demon world?

19. What do people with intelligence study (if they are Christians)?

20. "He assumed humanity that we might become God." Comment on this statement. Is it biblical?

21. What is happening to idolatry and Greek philosophy at this time (according to Athanasius)? When was Greek philosophy revived in the "Christian" universities?

22. If Christ is stopping the fraud of demons and displacing their rule in the world, what verses of the Bible come to mind concerning this?

On the Incarnation | Chapter 9 Worksheet 1 | Name

Study Questions

1. How did Athanasius come to know the truth?

2. What does Athanasius say will mark Christ's second coming?

3. How do we read the Scriptures rightly?

4. What marks a Christian according to Athanasius?

On the Incarnation | Essay | Name

ESSAY ASSIGNMENT Provide a 500-word essay on **one** of the following subject areas:

1. Write an essay on Athanasius' optimistic outlook on Christ's kingdom. What had been accomplished over the previous 300 years since Christ came to earth? How should this encourage our outlook today?

2. Write an essay on the apologetic Athanasius used against the skeptical Gentiles. How did he defend Christ's incarnation, resurrection, and present rule?

3. Write an essay on the marvelous characteristics of the Incarnation. What is the mystery of it? What did it accomplish? Why is it more impressive than any other religion?

| On the Incarnation | Exam | Scope: Athanasius | Total score: ____ of 100 | Name |

MULTIPLE CHOICE Circle all that apply. (5 points each)

1. To whom does Athanasius address this book?
   A. Church at Rome
   B. Theophilus
   C. Macarius
   D. Constantine

2. Which of the following was not a group addressed by Athanasius in this book?
   A. Gnostics
   B. Epicureans
   C. Platonists
   D. Aristotelians

3. What does Athanasius use as a symbol of faith in Christ's death? (More than one applies).
   A. Sign of the Cross
   B. Baptism
   C. Saying the Word "Christ"
   D. Taking the Lord's Supper

4. What is the center of our faith, according to Athanasius?
   A. The promises of God
   B. The incarnation
   C. The cross of Christ
   D. The resurrection of Christ

5. From what extra-biblical texts does Athansius quote? (More than one applies).
   A. Wisdom
   B. Maccabees
   C. Didache
   D. Shepherd of Hermes

TRUE/FALSE (6 points each)

6. ____ Athanasius addressed the Gnostics on the basis of New Testament Scripture.

7. ____ Athanasius had respect for Greek philosophy.

8. ____ Athanasius appealed to Plato's position in order to show the reasonableness of the incarnation for the Gentiles.

9. ____ Athanasius believed that the greatest exemplars of the Christian faith were martyrs and celibates.

10. ____ Athanasius believed that the Christian faith would be overcome by the Roman pagan ideas and powers.

SHORT ANSWER

11. What is the most depraved form of sin in a society according to Athanasius and Paul in Romans 1:27-31?

12. How did Christ compare to the Greek philosophers?

13. How do we know that Jesus was truly human?

14. How far had the Gospel gone at this time? (Name at least 3 countries)

Match the Following

1. Aesculapius

2. Dionysus

3. Gnostics

4. Epicureans

5. Platonists

6. Delphi

a. Those who believed the Creator God was not connected to the NT God

b. A place where many pagan oracles originated

c. The Greek that researched healing properties of plants

d. The Greek god that was the party god who promoted drunknness

e. Those who believed the universe was self-created and operates randomly.

f. Those who believed that God created the world out of pre-existent matter.

The Imitation of Christ — Book 1, Worksheet 1 — Name

VOCABULARY 1. Match the word with the correct definition

1. Contrition
2. Delusion
3. Laxity
4. Avaricious
5. Pretext
6. Vainglory
7. Reprobate

a. excessive elation or pride over one's own achievements, abilities, etc.; boastful vanity.
b. the state of being contrite.
c. the insatiable greed for riches; an inordinate, miserly desire to gain and hoard wealth.
d. a depraved, unprincipled, or wicked person.
e. something that is put forward to conceal a true purpose or object; an ostensible reason; excuse.
f. not strict or severe; careless or negligent.
g. something that is falsely or delusively believed or propagated.

VOCABULARY 2. Match the word with the correct definition

1. Irresolute
2. Fruition
3. Solace
4. Enamored
5. Penance
6. Salutary
7. Untrammeled

a. not confined, limited, or impeded.
b. comfort in sorrow, misfortune, or trouble; alleviation of distress or discomfort.
c. uncertain of how to act or proceed: vacillating.
d. promoting or conducive to some beneficial purpose; wholesome.
e. enjoyment, as of something attained or realized.
f. a punishment undergone in token of penitence for sin.
g. affected by strong feelings of love, admiration, or fascination.

VOCABULARY 3. Use each word in a sentence of your own construction

1. Enlightened –
   Your Sentence:

2. Contrition –
   Your Sentence:

58 Great Christian Classics: Four Essential Works of the Faith

3. Delusion –
   Your Sentence:

4. Sublime –
   Your Sentence:

5. Laxity –
   Your Sentence:

6. Avaricious –
   Your Sentence:

7. Fawn –
   Your Sentence:

8. Pretext –
   Your Sentence:

9. Vainglory –
   Your Sentence:

10. Reprobate –
    Your Sentence:

11. Irresolute –
    Your Sentence:

12. Fruition –
    Your Sentence:

13. Mortification –
    Your Sentence:

14. Solace –
    Your Sentence:

15. Enamored –
    Your Sentence:

16. Penance –
    Your Sentence:

17. Salutary –
    Your Sentence:

18. Untrammeled –
    Your Sentence:

| *The Imitation of Christ* | Book 1 Worksheet 2 | Name |

STUDY QUESTIONS

SECTION 1

1. Reference the first paragraph concerning the theme of this book. Is A'Kempis saying that we will be freed from blindness by walking with Christ? Or is he saying that we will be freed from blindness when we walk with Christ? Does A'Kempis' view agree with John 8:12? How does this comport with 2 Peter 1:5-9 and 2 Corinthians 4:4-6?

2. Where does A'Kempis place the authority of Scripture in comparison with the authority of the "Saints?"

3. What is more important than knowledge and discourses on doctrinal issues for A'Kempis?

4. What does the last paragraph mean when it says that we ought not to love things that are visible? Would it be wrong to love your father and mother, for example? Does he despise the visible, material world as a gnostic dualist might? How might he word this so that it would conform better to Colossians 3:2?

Note: Gnostic dualism taught that the material world was created by a lesser god and was therefore more contemptible or of lesser value and importance than the spiritual world.

Section 2

1. What does A'Kempis condemn about learned men and intellectualism? Do you see this sort of thing in some learning institutions today?

2. What does God expect of those who have knowledge? Reference James 1:22-27.

Section 3

1. Who is the Author of all things who speaks to us, and how does He speak to us?

2. A'Kempis speaks of the pure, simple, and stable life. What is this?

3. According to A'Kempis, what is God going to focus upon, and what is He not going to focus upon on the day of Judgment?

Section 4

1. What is A'Kempis' view of the nature of the mind? Is he optimistic or pessimistic? Is this biblical?

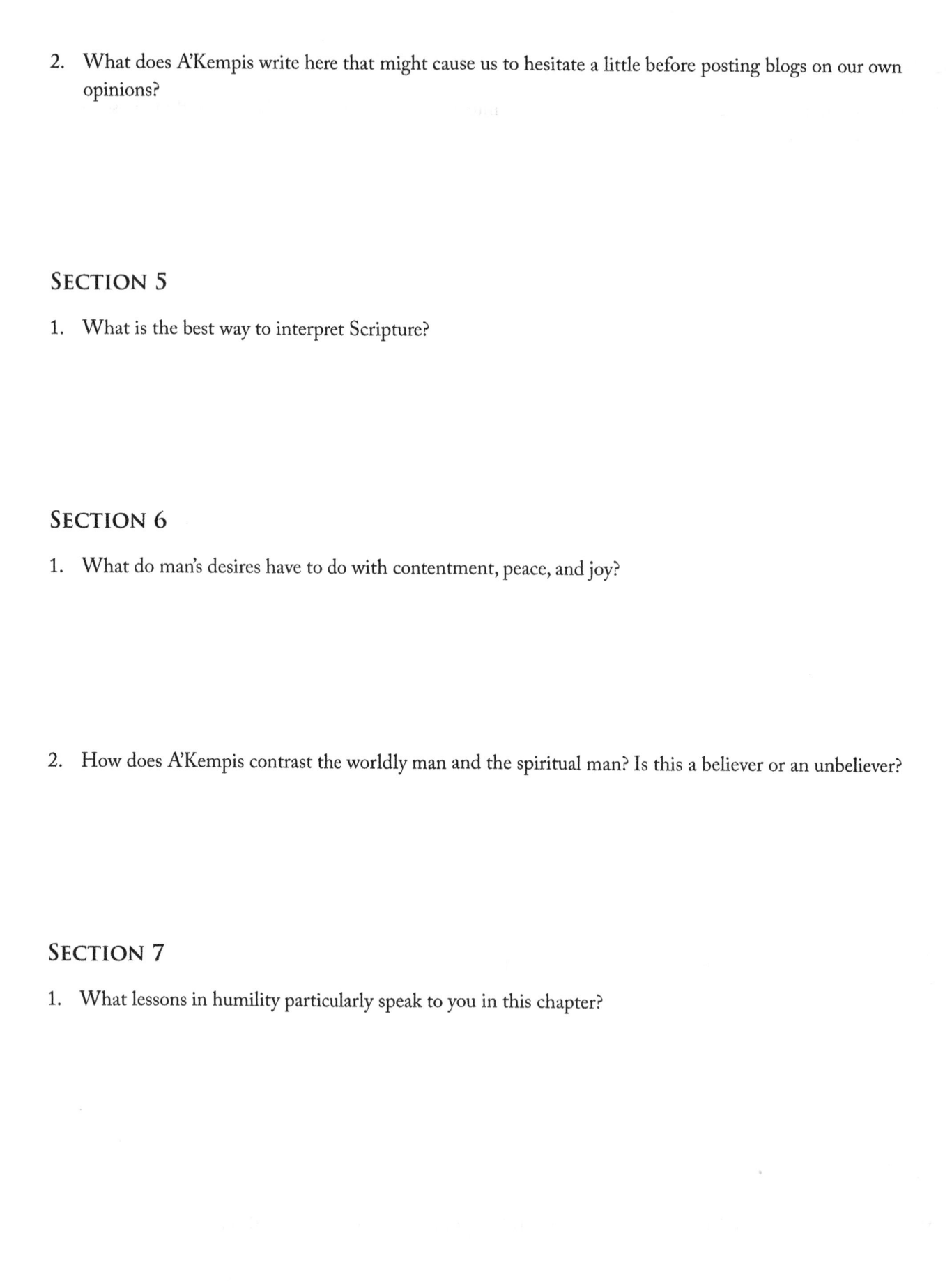

2. What does A'Kempis write here that might cause us to hesitate a little before posting blogs on our own opinions?

SECTION 5

1. What is the best way to interpret Scripture?

SECTION 6

1. What do man's desires have to do with contentment, peace, and joy?

2. How does A'Kempis contrast the worldly man and the spiritual man? Is this a believer or an unbeliever?

SECTION 7

1. What lessons in humility particularly speak to you in this chapter?

SECTION 8

1. Is this hesitation to establish familiar friendships a biblical idea? Throughout Christian history there were forms of asceticism where men would isolate themselves from other men for long periods of time. Could this have affected A'Kempis?

SECTION 9

1. Give a biblical proof text for the axiom, "It is safer to obey than to rule."

2. Is there a tendency for people to avoid any form of submission to church authority by "preference for other places and desire for change"? List a few areas where you might need to yield some of your opinions for the sake of peace in your church.

SECTION 10

1. Is avoiding all hospitality, feasting, and parties the best way to avoid gossip and idle talk? What guards does A'Kempis give to avoid the sins of the tongue?

SECTION 11

1. What is the greatest obstacle to our progress in the Christian life, according to A'Kempis? Do you agree or disagree? Why?

2. What is the relationship between God's grace and our effort in this chapter?

3. What is the spiritual battle described here?

SECTION 12

1. Why is adversity a good thing for the Christian man?

SECTION 13

1. How do you overcome temptation?

2. What is the value of temptation to the Christian?

3. Who was the poet Ovid? Was he a Christian or a non-Christian? How does A'Kempis quote him in this chapter?

4. What does A'Kempis say about the sovereignty of God over trials and over the salvation of a person in this chapter?

Section 14

1. Why are we so easily distressed when things don't go our way?

2. What is A'Kempis' view of original sin?

Section 15

1. Can the same deed be done with a good motivation or a bad motivation? What are the good motives and the bad motives listed in this chapter?

Section 16

1. Why should you deal with the faults and frailties of others?

SECTION 16

1. Why should you deal with the faults and frailties of others?

SECTION 17

1. What is a habit and a tonsure?

2. What can you learn about life in the monastery from this section?

3. Are there lessons contained in this section that any Christian might incorporate into his life though he lives at home and not in a monastery?

4. Is A'Kempis condemning all bodily passions as wrong? Are we never to seek anything in life but God?

SECTION 18

1. What holy fathers do you think A'Kempis is speaking of in this chapter?

2. How do you think he knows so much about the church fathers?

3. How does he use the word "perfect?" Compare with the King James Version's use of the word. Reference Genesis 6:9, 2 Timothy 3:17, esp. Ephesians 4:12,13

4. He seems to be complaining about the spiritual laxness of the times, especially within the monastery. What was the state of these monasteries at this time?

SECTION 19

1. Who determines what will happen? Man proposes, but what does God do?

2. Cultural Setting: What more can you learn about life in the monastery from this chapter?

SECTION 20

1. He quotes Seneca here in this section. Who was Seneca?

2. Does he have strong biblical backing for this exhortation to prefer solitude? Did the Apostle Paul live his life without going abroad and visiting with people?

SECTION 21

1. What is contrition and is there biblical support for it?

2. What is the proper role of contrition in our lives according to A'Kempis and Scripture?

3. What are the biblical doctrine of hell? What is the doctrine of purgatory?

SECTION 22

1. Who are the truly happy people according to A'Kempis?

2. What is the problem with the riches of this earth compared to what we will enjoy in heaven?

3. Does he believe that a man can be without sin in this life?

Section 23

1. "Happy and wise is he who endeavors to be during his life as he wishes to be found at his death." How would you like to be found the day of your death?

Section 24

1. Does sorrow cleanse the soul and make peace with God? Reference 1 John 1:9.

2. Does A'Kempis distinguish between hell and purgatory in this chapter?

3. From this chapter and the previous chapters, what is the motivation A'Kempis presents for obedience? Is he biblically balanced here? What is our motivation for fighting the good fight?

4. Is "live rightly and grieve for your sins" a good summary of the Christian life? Give biblical reference.

SECTION 25

1. Where does assurance of perseverance come from according to the story related in this chapter?

2. Who were the Carthusians and Cistercians?

3. What sorts of things should we enjoy above all others?

4. How does one achieve contentment with either poverty or riches?

The Imitation of Christ — Book 2, Worksheet 1 — Name

VOCABULARY 1. Match the word with the correct definition

1. Consolation
2. Wretched
3. Stigmata
4. Defamer
5. Sluggishness
6. Lax

a. to disgrace; bring dishonor upon.
b. to alleviate or lessen the grief, sorrow, or the disappointment of; give solace or comfort.
c. indisposed to action or exertion; lacking in energy; lazy; indolent.
d. not strict or severe; careless or negligent.
e. characterized by or attended with misery and sorrow.
f. a mark of disgrace or infamy; a stain or reproach, as on one's reputation.

VOCABULARY 2. Match the word with the correct definition

1. Presumptuous
2. Remedy
3. Resign
4. Contrite
5. Bliss
6. Infusion
7. Chalice

a. to submit (oneself, one's mind, etc.) without resistance.
b. steeping or soaking so as to extract the soluble properties or ingredients.
c. a drinking cup or goblet.
d. unwarrantedly or impertinently bold; forward.
e. filled with a sense of guilt and the desire for atonement; penitent.
f. something that cures.
g. supreme happiness; utter joy or contentment.

VOCABULARY 3. Use each word in a sentence of your own construction

1. Consolation –
   Your Sentence:

2. Wretched –
   Your Sentence:

3. Stigmata –

Great Christian Classics: Four Essential Works of the Faith

Your Sentence:

4. Defamer –
   Your Sentence:

5. Sluggishness –
   Your Sentence:

6. Lax –
   Your Sentence:

7. Presumptuous –
   Your Sentence:

8. Remedy –
   Your Sentence:

9. Resign –
   Your Sentence:

10. Contrite –
    Your Sentence:

11. Bliss –
    Your Sentence:

12. Infusion –
    Your Sentence:

13. Chalice –
    Your Sentence:

The Imitation of Christ — Book 2, Worksheet 2 — Name

STUDY QUESTIONS

SECTION 1

1. How does A'Kempis describe a living, personal relationship with Christ?

2. How does A'Kempis encourage you to bear up under suffering?

3. What gets in the way of inner peace and consolation?

SECTION 2

1. How do you get along with others and have peace with men?

SECTION 3

1. Describe a peaceful man as depicted in this chapter.

Section 4

1. What is the difference between purity and simplicity?

2. Is it accurate to say that a pure heart understands all things clearly and without difficulty?

Section 5

1. Why is A'Kempis very hesitant to criticize others?

Section 6

1. How does one achieve a life of peace and joy according to this chapter?

Section 7

1. How does A'Kempis describe a relationship with Christ?

Section 8

1. When A'Kempis refers to Jesus as a rich treasure, which biblical passage is he drawing upon?

2. He speaks of losing God's grace in two places here. Is he referring to losing your salvation?

SECTION 9

1. Who was Laurence the Martyr, and what was his relationship with Sixtus?

2. How you handle the comforting, easy times should help you when things start getting tough. How should you accept the comforting times?

3. What do you do when God withholds His grace and comfort?

4. According to A'Kempis, does this withdrawal of the grace of God happen to every saint?

SECTION 10

1. What surpasses all worldly pleasure?

2. What hinders heavenly visitations?

SECTION 11

1. What kind of love would A'Kempis call a genuine love of Christ?

2. What is the "one thing needful"?

SECTION 12

1. What are the two ways taken by men as described in this chapter?

2. What are the benefits of being "in the Cross?"

3. What is the way of the Cross?

4. At what point can you say that you have found paradise on earth?

5. Is this a realistic portrayal of the Christian life? Is this the kind of life that most professing Christians seek after in our time?

The Imitation of Christ — Book 3, Worksheet 1 — Name

VOCABULARY 1. Match the word with the correct definition

1. Seducers
2. Circumspect
3. Incentive
4. Enshroud
5. Expedient
6. Insolently

a. a means devised or employed in an exigency; resource; shift.
b. boldly rude or disrespectful; contemptuously impertinent; insulting.
c. to lead astray, as from duty, rectitude, or the like; corrupt.
d. to shroud; conceal.
e. watchful and discreet; cautious; prudent.
f. something that incites or tends to incite to action or a greater effort, as a reward offered for increased productivity.

VOCABULARY 2. Match the word with the correct definition

1. Supernal
2. Equanimity
3. Transitory
4. Advert
5. Irrevocably
6. Disparagement
7. Assuage

a. not to be revoked or recalled; unable to be repealed or annulled; unalterable.
b. to soothe, calm, or mollify.
c. to depreciate by indirect means: speak slightingly about.
d. not lasting, enduring, permanent, or eternal.
e. to turn the attention.
f. mental or emotional stability or composure, especially under tension or strain; calmness; equilibrium.
g. being in or belonging to the heaven of divine beings; heavenly, celestial, or divine.

VOCABULARY 3. Use each word in a sentence of your own construction

1. Seducers –
   Your Sentence:

2. Circumspect –
   Your Sentence:

Great Christian Classics: Four Essential Works of the Faith 81

3. Incentive –
   Your Sentence:

4. Complacency –
   Your Sentence:

5. Enshroud –
   Your Sentence:

6. Unfathomable –
   Your Sentence:

7. Expedient –
   Your Sentence:

8. Dispose –
   Your Sentence:

9. Renounce –
   Your Sentence:

10. Insolently –
    Your Sentence:

11. Supernal –
    Your Sentence:

12. Equanimity –
    Your Sentence:

13. Transitory –
    Your Sentence:

14. Advert –
    Your Sentence:

15. Festive –
    Your Sentence:

16. Peevish –
    Your Sentence:

The Imitation of Christ — Book 3, Worksheet 2

STUDY QUESTIONS

SECTION 1

1. How does Christ speak to us?

SECTION 2

1. A'Kempis distinguishes between the "speaking" of Moses and the prophets and the "speaking" of God. Explain the distinction.

2. What happens to someone who hears God's Word but does not do it?

SECTION 3

1. What is the complaint that Christ brings in this chapter?

2. What is the purpose of placing this conversation between Christ and the disciple into this reading?

Section 4

1. What is A'Kempis' view of devotional books, pictures, and visible signs and representations? Could this include pictures of Christ and visible symbols like the cross?

2. What does Christ tell us our good deeds do for us?

Section 5

1. What are the differences between the definition of love Paul provides in 1 Corinthians 13 and A'Kempis' definitions?

2. Does A'Kempis believe in God's sovereignty? Defend your point from examples in this chapter.

Section 6

1. Why does the Lord consider the disciple weak in his love here?

2. What does A'Kempis mean by "the veneration of the saints"? Does he consider this an important part of the Christian life? What does the Bible say about honoring the saints who have gone before us?

Section 7

1. What is A'Kempis concerned about in this chapter?

2. How does A'Kempis contrast our attitude toward times of peace and times of trial?

Section 8

1. How does A'Kempis view life in this chapter?

Section 9

1. What happens to those who glory in themselves or in something besides God?

2. Does this chapter convict you in any way, and how?

Section 10

1. How does God show His love for us according to this section?

2. Do you think this chapter applies only to the monk who secludes himself in a monastery, or could it apply to anybody? Explain.

SECTION 11

1. What is Christ's concern relating to the disciple in this chapter?

2. In what sense does A'Kempis use the term "flesh" in this chapter?

SECTION 12

1. How does A'Kempis' Christ encourage the man to endure trials in this soliloquy?

SECTION 13

1. In what phrase does A'Kempis equate the sinful flesh to the body in this chapter?

2. How does Christ encourage us to submit to earthly authorities (fathers, pastors, elders) in this section?

3. Might some parts of this offend those who feel it is important for men to retain a "self-esteem"? Does A'Kempis go too far in encouraging us to be humble here?

SECTION 14

1. Does A'Kempis think that man is able to save himself? Explain using examples from this chapter.

SECTION 15

1. What might you say to one who tells you that "the Spirit prompted me to do this or that"?

2. When A'Kempis speaks of conforming ourselves to the will of God, what will does he refer to—God's moral law and direction or God's decreed purpose?

SECTION 16

1. The phrase "Use temporal things but desire heavenly things" is an excellent summary of A'Kempis' view of earthly pleasures. Explain what he means by this. Do you agree or disagree?

Section 17

1. How is it that tribulations do not harm the Christian?

Section 18

1. A'Kempis' theology of the Old and New Testaments is seen in this section. How would you summarize it? What are the differences between the Old Testament saints and the New Testament saints?

Section 19

1. Is Christ remonstrating or rebuking the disciple here? What is the issue of concern?

2. How is suffering made "easy"?

Section 20

1. What weakness(es) does the disciple confess in this section?

2. What is A'Kempis saying about life here? Should we love life?

Section 21

1. Does such loving language as you found in this chapter sound strange, especially when one speaks of a Friend with whom they have never met face to face? Is it appropriate language? Can you find biblical examples of such language?

2. A'Kempis speaks of liberty and freedom in this chapter. But to what are we fettered? From what must we be freed?

Section 22

1. When A'Kempis refers to "merit" in this chapter, he calls it a gift. How can something merited be a gift?

2. What kind of people does God choose for His friends?

Section 23

1. Give biblical reference for the summary statements of the way to peace and true liberty.

Section 24

1. What sort of things disturb us unnecessarily?

Section 25

1. In what does the perfection of a man consist?

Section 26

1. What is disorderly affection?

2. According to A'Kempis, what is God's Law relating to bodily pleasures? Do you agree?

Section 27

1. What should you do with earthly goods and honors according to this chapter?

Section 28

1. Why shouldn't you be bothered by other people's opinions of you?

Section 30

1. Why is the disciple so slow to turn to God in prayer when he is in need?

2. Why does God send us trials or withdraw blessings from us?

Section 31

1. What is it to separate ourselves entirely from that which is transitory and created?

Section 32

1. What are the sorts of things that make us unsettled and discontented in life?

2. What is true heavenly wisdom as portrayed in this chapter?

Section 33

1. What is it that makes us changeable and moody?

Section 34

1. What is the disciple struggling with in this chapter?

Section 35

1. What sort of life does the Christian live in this world?

2. How do we survive this battle?

Section 36

1. How do you deal with false accusations?

2. Why would Paul answer his accusers?

Section 37

1. What is pure and entire resignation to God? Is it biblical?

Section 38

1. What is freedom as defined here and how do you get it?

2. How does one stay out of trouble?

Section 39

1. How does A'Kempis affirm the sovereignty of God in this section?

Section 40

1. How does A'Kempis describe man's basic nature apart from the grace of God?

2. What do you think provokes A'Kempis' reference to the Jews in this chapter?

Section 41

1. How is inner peace achieved according to this chapter?

Section 42

1. Does A'Kempis present it as a virtue not to weep upon the abandonment or death of friends? Is this biblical?

2. Does A'Kempis recommend friendships here? How should we establish friendships?

Section 43

1. How do you attain good knowledge and wisdom?

Section 44

1. Why does the Lord commend "ignorance" in this section?

Section 45

1. How does A'Kempis describe men in this chapter? Do you believe it to be an accurate description?

2. How does he describe this life that we live?

Section 46

1. How should you handle yourself when others slander you?

Section 47

1. What makes our life worth living and the spiritual struggles and humiliation we go through worthwhile?

Section 48

1. What two realities are contrasted in this chapter?

2. Where do your thoughts tend to gravitate?

Section 49

1. What are the extenuating conditions that make it hard to obey?

2. Does the Bible require that we submit ourselves to the will of everyone? Is that what A'Kempis is saying in this chapter?

SECTION 50

1. How does A'Kempis affirm the absolute sovereignty of God in this section?

SECTION 51

1. What seems to be A'Kempis' highest duty for man? Is this a biblical assessment?

SECTION 52

1. In what sense might this be considered a more "evangelical" chapter?

SECTION 53

1. What is the root of all vices described here?

2. Is denying oneself equal to the rooting out of self-love?

SECTION 54

1. What is "nature" and "grace" in this comparison between the movements of nature and grace?

2. List a few of the contrasts A'Kempis draws between nature and grace.

SECTION 55

1. What is A'Kempis' perspective concerning natural man (absent of the grace of God), as revealed in this section? Is there biblical substantiation for this?

SECTION 56

1. A'Kempis uses antithetic parallelism in this chapter. Give several examples. (Antithetic Parallelism: in which the second member of a line [or verse] gives the obverse side of the same thought.)

SECTION 57

1. In this section, there seems to be a little satire. Give an example or two. Is this characteristic of Christ?

2. How is a mature man characterized in this section?

Section 58

1. What are the sorts of judgments considered incomprehensible and forbidden to be tampered with recorded here in this section?

2. How does A'Kempis' view of God's sovereign grace trump his view of merit in this chapter?

Section 59

1. What is our chief desire?

The Imitation of Christ   Book 4 Worksheet 1   Name

VOCABULARY 1. Match the word with the correct definition

1. Commemoration
2. Vices
3. Jubilation
4. Deplored
5. Inflame

6. Condescension

a. an immoral or evil habit or practice.
b. to arouse to a high degree of passion or feeling.
c. to feel or express deep grief for or in regard to.
d. to honor the memory of by some observance.
e. to behave as if one is conscious of descending from a superior position, rank, or dignity.
f. a feeling of or the expression of joy or exultation.

VOCABULARY 2. Match the word with the correct definition

1. Indolence
2. Superabundance
3. Enmeshed
4. Suppliant
5. Relish
6. Eucharist
7. Ardent

a. expressive of supplication, as words, actions, etc.
b. having or showing a disposition to avoid exertion; slothful.
c. exceedingly or excessively abundant; more than sufficient; excessive.
d. to take pleasure in; like; enjoy.
e. having, expressive of, or characterized by intense feeling; passionate; fervent.
f. to catch, as in a net; entangle.
g. another term often used for communion; meaning, thanksgiving.

VOCABULARY 3. Use each word in a sentence of your own construction

1. Commemoration –
   Your Sentence:

2. Vices –
   Your Sentence:

3. Jubilation –
   Your Sentence:

4. Deplored –
   Your Sentence:

5. Salutary –
   Your Sentence:

6. Inflame –
   Your Sentence:

7. Condescension –
   Your Sentence:

8. Indolence –
   Your Sentence:

   Superabundance –
   Your Sentence:

10. Enmeshed –
    Your Sentence:

11. Suppliant –
    Your Sentence:

12. Relish –
    Your Sentence:

13. Eucharist –
    Your Sentence:

14. Ardent –
    Your Sentence:

15. Blissful –
    Your Sentence:

The Imitation of Christ | Book 4 Worksheet 2 | Name

Study Questions

Section 1

1. What does A'Kempis believe concerning the relationship between the Lord's Table and the body of Christ?

2. What examples does A'Kempis give of those who valued worshiping God and communing with Him in His temple? How does he apply this to himself?

3. How does A'Kempis tie in the honoring of the saints and relics to the worship of God?

4. What is A'Kempis' main complaint in this chapter?

Section 2

1. What method does A'Kempis use to highlight our unworthiness for this salvation?

2. Does A'Kempis believe in transubstantiation? (Note: Transubstantiation is the change of the substance of the bread and wine into the body and blood of Christ at the Table.)

Section 3

1. What is the argument here concerning taking communion on a regular basis?

2. What frequency does A'Kempis recommend or practice the table himself?

3. What is A'Kempis' attitude in receiving the Lord's Table?

Section 4

1. Does every person who takes the sacrament obtain great gifts from God?

2. What blessings does A'Kempis believe are shared at the Table?

Section 5

1. What insight do you receive from A'Kempis' view of the priesthood and the celebration of the Mass? How "Roman Catholic" is A'Kempis?

Section 6

1. What is the conundrum the disciple faces in this short chapter?

2. Do these meditations strengthen our faith or weaken it?

Section 7

1. Would a Protestant have problems with this chapter?

Section 8

1. What does Christ ask in this chapter? Does this have a biblical basis?

Section 9

1. How did Christ redeem us?

2. How does A'Kempis view his own works here?

3. What is the expiatory sacrifice and the offering of propitiation, and who offers it here?

SECTION 10

1. What impedes your communion with Christ?

2. How do you cleanse yourself? What is the difference between spitting out the poison and applying the remedy?

3. Why do people stay away from the table?

SECTION 11

1. Will we need a sacrament in heaven? Why or why not?

2. What else do we have for comfort and guidance along the way besides communion?

3. What admonitions does A'Kempis provide for priests?

Section 12

1. How does one prepare for the table?

Section 13

1. This chapter contains an apologetic for the Christian faith itself. Explain.

Section 14

1. How is the disciple convicted of his coldness at the table?

2. What should you do if your heart is not similarly filled with love for Christ?

Section 15

1. What sorts of things hinder our devotion?

2. What should you do when your heart is cold to Christ?

Section 16

1. Is this a regenerate man speaking? What would cause you to think that this man is yet to be regenerated?

Section 17

1. What examples are we given in this chapter of those who humbly received the Savior?

2. What two desires are brought together in the final paragraph of the chapter?

Section 17

1. What examples are we given in this chapter of those who humbly received the Savior?

2. What two desires are brought together in the final paragraph of the chapter?

Section 18

1. How does this chapter speak directly to the long standing controversy that has surrounded the Lord's table?

2. Does A'Kempis sound more like Augustine and Anselm, or Aquinas in the final paragraph?

| *The Imitation of Christ* | Essay | Name |

ESSAY ASSIGNMENT Provide a 500-word essay on **one** of the following subject areas.

1. What emphasis does A'Kempis place upon the sovereignty of God regenerating hearts, giving faith, and working in us to will and to do of His good pleasure? Does his emphasis upon man's contribution to walking with Christ overshadow the biblical teaching on the sovereignty of God?

2. How much does A'Kempis' respect for Scripture contribute to the Protestant Reformation? Does he really root his ideas in Scripture? How did it compare to the way Scripture was handled in the universities/seminaries of his day?

3. A'Kempis uses the word "merit" throughout his writings. How does he speak of merit? Is it biblical to think of God's blessings as merited? How would the Reformers feel about his view of merit? How would the decisions of the Council of Trent align with A'Kempis' views?

4. A'Kempis refers to the Apocryphal books throughout his writings. Identify several examples where he does this. Research the history of the biblical canon between AD 500 and AD 1600.

5. How does this little book differ from the Puritan writings such as John Bunyan's *Pilgrim's Progress* or Richard Baxter's *A Christian Directory* or Thomas Watson's *Heaven Taken by Storm*? How is it similar?

6. One of the important virtues that A'Kempis commends throughout the book is "detachment from this world and the creatures of this world." Was Jesus detached from this world? Were the Apostles detached from the world? What does the Bible say about our relationship with the world? You will need to interact with various definitions of "world."

7. What sort of Roman Catholic doctrines are contained in the book? Which Roman Catholic doctrines are not addressed? What does this say about A'Kempis' theology? Is he closer to the Protestants or to the Roman Catholics? At what points does he sound evangelical? Does he describe our relationship to God primarily as membership in a Church or as a personal relationship with Jesus Christ?

8. Was A'Kempis a true Christian, a man of true faith? Answering this question will define the bounds of ecumenicity for Protestant Christians and is worthy of much careful thought and consideration.

9. What part does the Law of God play in A'Kempis' portrayal of Christian piety? Do you find the Ten Commandments in the books? What is his ethic for life?

The Imitation of Christ	Exam	Scope: A'Kempis	Total score: ____ of 100	Name

MULTIPLE CHOICE Circle all that apply. (5 points each)

1. In what years did A'Kempis live?
   A. 1440-1531
   B. 1380-1471
   C. 1300-1390
   D. 1321-1401

2. What frequency of communion does A'Kempis recommend?
   A. Daily
   B. Weekly
   C. Monthly
   D. Twice a day

3. What does A'Kempis mean by the "imitation of Christ"?
   A. Teaching what Jesus taught
   B. Keeping the commandments of God
   C. Believing in Jesus Christ
   D. Following Jesus by following his example

4. What is the practice of tonsure?
   A. Wearing of a robe
   B. Going to Confession
   C. Clipping of one's hair around the scalp
   D. Making Monastic vows

5. According to A'Kempis, what must accompany knowledge (more than one apply)?
   A. Fear of God
   B. Love
   C. Compassion
   D. Humility

6. When reading the Scriptures, what are we to look for instead of "fair phrases"?
   A. Commandments
   B. Doctrine
   C. Truth
   D. Examples

7. According to A'Kempis, what should we do instead of spending time in fruitless discussion?
   A. Serve others in need
   B. Meditate upon truth in solitude
   C. Give money to the poor
   D. Spend time in the church

8. A'Kempis says that there are many who "love his kingdom, but few who..."
   A. care for those in need
   B. are truly humble
   C. bear His cross
   D. read the Scriptures

9. According to A'Kempis, what is a brave lover?
   A. A brave lover stands firm in temptation
   B. A brave lover is selfless
   C. A brave lover protects others
   D. A brave lover is not afraid of others

True/False

1. ____ A'Kempis believed the doctrine of Purgatory.

2. ____ A'Kempis believed that priests should wear vestments.

3. ____ A'Kempis is pessimistic concerning the natural state of fallen man (including the mind of man).

4. ____ A'Kempis believed that doctrine was not important in the Christian life.

5. ____ A'Kempis believed that we should submit reason to faith when it comes to the mysteries of the faith.

6. ____ A'Kempis believed that the monastic life was unhelpful to the Christian.

7. ____ A'Kempis refers to the Apocryphal books in *The Imitation of Christ*.

Match the Following

1. Carthusians   a. A Roman Stoic philosopher

2. Cistercians   b. A deacon in the Roman church, AD 258.

3. Seneca   c. White monks that emphasized manual labor

4. Lawrence the Martyr   A sect that rejected the material world as "evil"

5. Gnostics   e. An order of Bruno of Cologne, emphasizing silence

Short Answer

1. According to A'Kempis, what is the problem with learned men and intellectualism in the universities?

2. When A'Kempis teaches us to submit reason to faith in the final section of the book, what Christian authors does he follow in making this argument?

3. What does A'Kempis teach about the sovereignty of God?

The Institutes of the Christian Religion — Book 1, Chapter 1, Worksheet 1 — Name

VOCABULARY 1. Match the word with the correct definition

1. Contemplate
2. Confines (noun)
3. Infinitude
4. Subsistence
5. Impotence
6. Refulgence
7. Endued
8. Demigods

a. a radiant or resplendent quality or state.
b. an infinite extent, amount, or number.
c. to invest or endow with some gift, quality, or faculty.
d. the condition of remaining in existence.
e. to view or consider with continued attention.
f. lack of power, strength, or vigor.
g. a person so outstanding as to seem to approach the divine.
h. something (such as borders or walls) that encloses.

VOCABULARY 2. Use each word in a sentence of your own construction

1. Contemplate –
   Your Sentence:

2. Confines –
   Your Sentence:

3. Infinitude –
   Your Sentence:

4. Subsistence –
   Your Sentence:

Impotence –
Your Sentence:

6. Refulgence –
Your Sentence:

7. Endued –
Your Sentence:

8. Demigods –
Your Sentence:

The Institutes of the Christian Religion | Book 1, Chapter 1 Worksheet 2 | Name

STUDY QUESTIONS

1. How does knowing yourself help you to know about God?

2. How does knowing God help you to know about yourself?

3. Does Calvin intend to talk first about the knowledge of God or the knowledge of ourselves?

The Institutes of the Christian Religion Book 1, Chapter 2 Worksheet 1 Name

VOCABULARY 1. Match the word with the correct definition

1. Apprehend
2. Interpose
3. Frigid
4. Clemency
5. Promiscuously
6. Ostentatious

a. to place in an intervening position.
b. to grasp the meaning of; understand, especially intuitively; perceive.
c. characterized by or given to pretentious or conspicuous show in an attempt to impress others.
d. unemotional or unimaginative; lacking passion, sympathy, or sensitivity.
e. a disposition to be merciful and especially to moderate the severity of punishment due.
f. casual; irregular; haphazard.

VOCABULARY 2. Use each word in a sentence of your own construction

1. Apprehend –
   Your Sentence:

2. Interpose –
   Your Sentence:

3. Frigid –
   Your Sentence:

4. Clemency –
   Your Sentence:

5. Promiscuously –
   Your Sentence:

6. Ostentatious –
   Your Sentence:

The Institutes of the Christian Religion — Book 1, Chapter 2, Worksheet 2 — Name

Study Questions

1. Can we know God without worshiping God? Why or why not?

2. If the natural world shows God to be the Creator, what does Scripture show God to be? How is this reflected by the table of contents in Calvin's *Institutes*?

3. What is piety by Calvin's definition?

4. Is the following statement true or false? Explain your answer.
   "Calvin is trying to describe what the essence of God is, apart from the relationship God has with mankind."

5. What ought to be the two results of knowledge of God?

6. According to Calvin, what is "pure and true religion"?

The Institutes of the Christian Religion — Book 1, Chapter 3 | Worksheet 1 | Name

VOCABULARY 1. Match the word with the correct definition

1. Endued
2. Haughtiness
3. Tacit

a. blatantly and disdainfully proud.
b. implied or indicated (as by an act or by silence) but not actually expressed.
c. to invest or endow with some gift, quality, or faculty.

VOCABULARY 2. Use each word in a sentence of your own construction

1. Endued –
   Your Sentence:

2. Haughtiness –
   Your Sentence:

3. Tacit –
   Your Sentence:

The Institutes of the Christian Religion — Book 1, Chapter 3, Worksheet 2 — Name

Study Questions

1. What does the existence of idol worship prove?

The Institutes of the Christian Religion — Book 1, Chapter 4, Worksheet 1 — Name

VOCABULARY 1. Match the word with the correct definition

1. Abyss
2. Bewitched
3. Licentious
4. Caprice

5. Loquaciously
6. Disparagement

7. Preposterous
8. Propensity
9. Expiation

10. Stupefaction
11. Execrable
12. Tribunal

13. Luxuriate

14. Oblivion

a. to enjoy oneself without stint; revel.
b. characterized by excessive talk; wordy.
c. to make stupid, groggy, or insensible.
d. to bring reproach or discredit upon; lower the estimation of.
e. a place or seat of judgment.
f. the condition or state of being forgotten or unknown.
g. lacking legal or moral restraints.
h. intellectual or moral depths.
i. a sudden, impulsive, and seemingly unmotivated notion or action.
j. a natural inclination or tendency.
k. utterly detestable; abominable; abhorrent.
l. the means by which atonement or reparation is made.
m. completely contrary to nature, reason, or common sense; absurd; senseless; utterly foolish.
n. to enchant; charm; fascinate.

VOCABULARY 2. Use each word in a sentence of your own construction

1. Abyss –
   Your Sentence:

2. Bewitch –
   Your Sentence:

3. Licentious –
   Your Sentence:

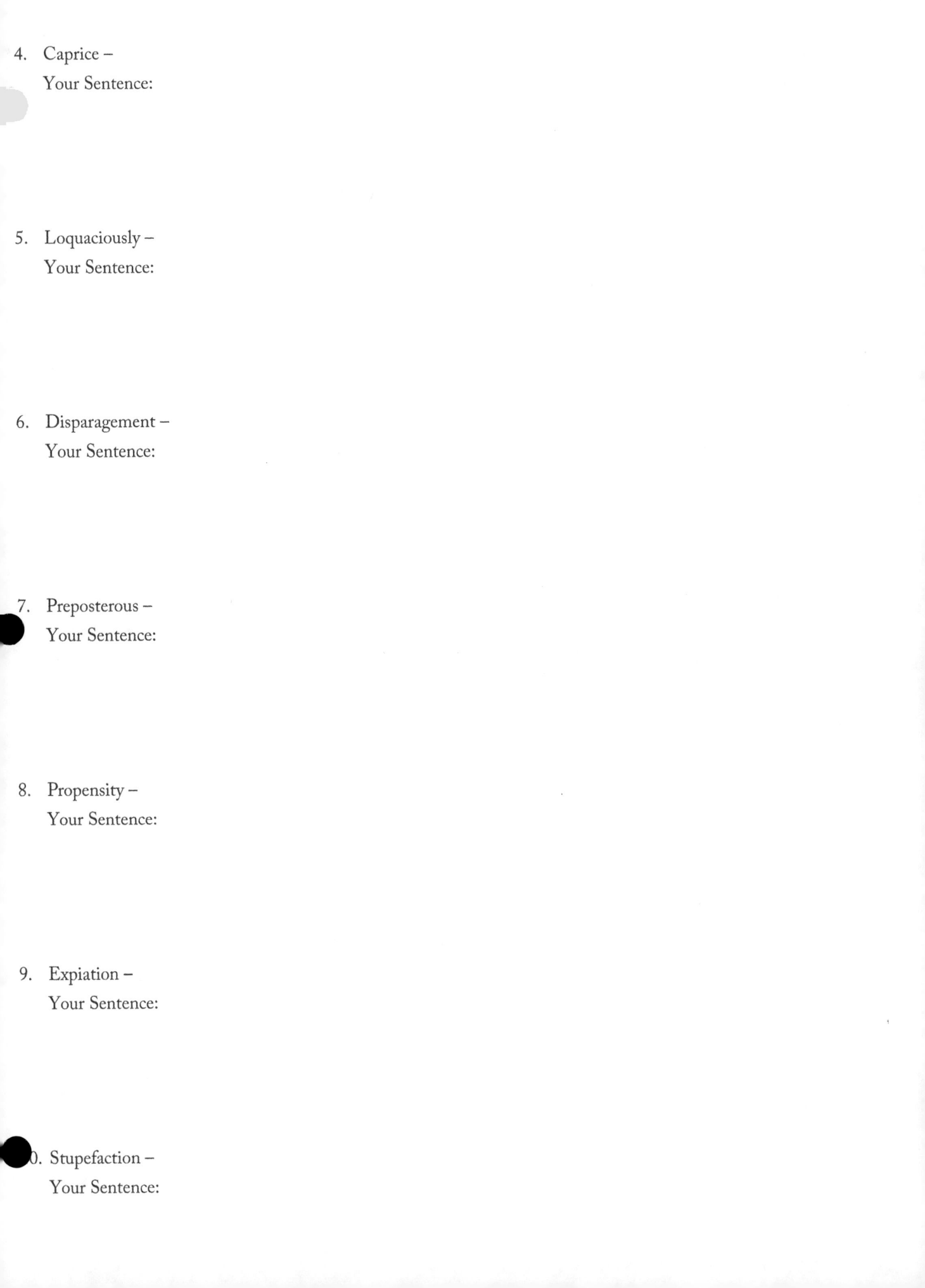

4. Caprice –
   Your Sentence:

5. Loquaciously –
   Your Sentence:

6. Disparagement –
   Your Sentence:

7. Preposterous –
   Your Sentence:

8. Propensity –
   Your Sentence:

9. Expiation –
   Your Sentence:

10. Stupefaction –
    Your Sentence:

11. Execrable –
    Your Sentence:

12. Tribunal –
    Your Sentence:

13. Luxuriate –
    Your Sentence:

14. Oblivion –
    Your Sentence:

The Institutes of the Christian Religion — Book 1, Chapter 4, Worksheet 2 — Name

STUDY QUESTIONS

1. What does Calvin mean by "foolish" and "stupid"? Is he talking about intelligence?

2. Is it the fool's fault that he is being foolish?

The Institutes of the Christian Religion — Book 1, Chapter 5, Worksheet 1 — Name

VOCABULARY 1. Match the word with the correct definition

1. Refulgent
2. Felicity
3. Obtuse
4. Depraved

a. the state of being happy, especially to a high degree; bliss.
b. marked by corruption or evil.
c. a radiant or resplendent quality or state.
d. not quick or alert in perception, feeling, or intellect; not sensitive or observant; dull.

VOCABULARY 2. Use each word in a sentence of your own construction

1. Refulgent –
   Your Sentence:

2. Felicity –
   Your Sentence:

3. Obtuse –
   Your Sentence:

4. Depraved –
   Your Sentence:

The Institutes of the Christian Religion | Book 1, Chapter 5, Worksheet 2 | Name

STUDY QUESTIONS

1. How is the world like a mirror?

2. In what way can creation's testimony concerning God be considered as "vain"?

3. "We cannot plead ignorance, without being condemned by our own consciences of laziness and ingratitude." How is ignorance related to ingratitude?

The Institutes of the Christian Religion — Book 1, Chapter 6, Worksheet 1 — Name

VOCABULARY 1. Match the word with the correct definition

1. Dissipate
2. Defective
3. Labyrinth

a. any confusingly intricate state of things or events; a bewildering complex.
b. to scatter in various directions; disperse; dispel.
c. having a flaw: imperfect in form, structure, or function.

VOCABULARY 2. Use each word in a sentence of your own construction

1. Dissipate –
   Your Sentence:

2. Defective –
   Your Sentence:

3. Labyrinth –
   Your Sentence:

The Institutes of the Christian Religion — Book 1, Chapter 6, Worksheet 2 — Name

Study Questions

1. How is Scripture like a pair of eye glasses?

2. "True and complete faith" and "sound knowledge" originate in what?

The Institutes of the Christian Religion — Book 1, Chapter 7, Worksheet 1 — Name

VOCABULARY 1. Match the word with the correct definition

1. Cunning
2. Cavil
3. Transcendent
4. Effrontery
5. Acquiesce
6. Obstreperous
7. Alacrity
8. Subjoins

a. to place in sequence or juxtaposition to something else.
b. to assent tacitly; submit or comply silently or without protest; agree; consent.
c. cheerful readiness, promptness, or willingness.
d. characterized by wiliness and trickery.
e. noisy, clamorous, or boisterous.
f. going beyond ordinary limits; surpassing; exceeding.
g. shameless or impudent boldness; barefaced audacity.
h. a trivial and annoying objection.

VOCABULARY 2. Use each word in a sentence of your own construction

1. Cunning –
   Your Sentence:

2. Cavil –
   Your Sentence:

3. Transcendent –
   Your Sentence:

4. Effrontery –
   Your Sentence:

5. Acquiesce –
   Your Sentence:

6. Obstreperous –
   Your Sentence:

7. Alacrity –
   Your Sentence:

8. Subjoins –
   Your Sentence:

The Institutes of the Christian Religion — Book 1, Chapter 7, Worksheet 2

STUDY QUESTIONS

1. Does Scripture prove itself to be God's Word?

2. How do we know Scripture is God's Word spoken to us?

3. Why are humility and submission required to believe Scripture?

The Institutes of the Christian Religion — Book 1, Chapter 9, Worksheet 1 — Name

VOCABULARY 1. Match the word with the correct definition

1. Superstitious
2. Supersede
3. Infallible
4. Repugnant
5. Imbued

a. distasteful, objectionable, or offensive.
b. absolutely trustworthy or sure.
c. to impregnate or inspire, as with feelings, opinions, etc.
d. to set aside or cause to be set aside as void, useless, or obsolete.
e. of, relating to, or swayed by superstition.

VOCABULARY 2. Use each word in a sentence of your own construction

1. Superstitious –
   Your Sentence:

2. Supersede –
   Your Sentence:

3. Infallible –
   Your Sentence:

4. Repugnant –
   Your Sentence:

5. Imbued –
   Your Sentence:

Great Christian Classics: Four Essential Works of the Faith

The Institutes of the Christian Religion — Book 1, Chapter 9, Worksheet 2 | Name

STUDY QUESTIONS

1. How do we detect false spirits? How do we know if the testimony we are hearing is that of the Spirit of God?

2. Calvin says: *"The Lord has intertwined the truth of his Word and his Spirit in such a way that we respect the Word when the Spirit illumines it, enabling us to see God's face, and we welcome the Spirit, with no risk of error, when we recognize him in his Word."*
What if someone's reaction is: "Isn't this circular reasoning? If it takes the testimony of the Spirit to believe the Word but it takes trusting the Word to verify the right Spirit—then which comes first, believing the Word or the Spirit?" What is your reaction?

The Institutes of the Christian Religion   Book 1 Chapter 13 Worksheet 1   Name

VOCABULARY 1. Match the word with the correct definition

1. Oracle
2. Expositor
3. Soberness
4. Evanescent
5. Epithets
6. Calumny
7. Puerile
8. Derogates

a. the act of uttering false charges or misrepresentations maliciously calculated to harm another's reputation.
b. vanishing; fading away; fleeting.
c. childishly foolish; immature or trivial.
d. a person who delivers authoritative, wise, or highly regarded and influential pronouncements.
e. a characterizing word or phrase accompanying or occurring in place of the name of a person or thing.
f. a person who expounds or gives an exposition.
g. to detract, as from authority, estimation.
h. marked by sedate or gravely or earnestly thoughtful character or demeanor.

VOCABULARY 2. Use each word in a sentence of your own construction

1. Oracle –
   Your Sentence:

2. Expositor –
   Your Sentence:

3. Soberness –
   Your Sentence:

4. Evanescent –
   Your Sentence:

5. Epithets –
   Your Sentence:

6. Calumny –
   Your Sentence:

7. Puerile –
   Your Sentence:

8. Derogates –
   Your Sentence:

The Institutes of the Christian Religion

Book 1
Chapter 13
Worksheet 2

Name

Study Questions

1. According to Augustine, when is Jesus called "God" and when is He called "the Son?"

2. What is Calvin's "helpful idea" in the last paragraph of the chapter?

The Institutes of the Christian Religion

Book 1
Chapter 14
Worksheet 1

Name

VOCABULARY 1. Match the word with the correct definition

1. Copious
2. Splendid
3. Evanescent
4. Compendious
5. Antecedent

a. gorgeous; magnificent; sumptuous.
b. vanishing; fading away; fleeting.
c. a preceding circumstance, event, object, style, phenomenon, etc.
d. marked by a brief expression of a comprehensive matter: concise and comprehensive.
e. exhibiting abundance or fullness, as of thoughts or words.

VOCABULARY 2. Use each word in a sentence of your own construction

1. Copious –
   Your Sentence:

2. Splendid –
   Your Sentence:

3. Evanescent –
   Your Sentence:

4. Compendious –
   Your Sentence:

5. Antecedent –
   Your Sentence:

The Institutes of the Christian Religion

Book 1
Chapter 14
Worksheet 2

Name

STUDY QUESTIONS

1. Summarize, in your own words, the two ways Calvin suggests for the reader to be sure he understands the character of God as the Creator.

The Institutes of the Christian Religion | Book 1 Chapter 15 Worksheet 1 | Name

VOCABULARY 1. Match the word with the correct definition

1. Specimen
2. Subterfuge
3. Deformity
4. Impugn
5. Effaced
6. Heterogenous
7. Expostulate

a. to assail by words or arguments: oppose or attack as false or lacking integrity.

b. different in kind; unlike; incongruous.

c. an artifice or expedient used to evade a rule, escape a consequence, hide something, etc.

d. the quality or state of being deformed, disfigured, or misshapen.

e. an individual, item, or part considered typical of a group, class, or whole.

f. to reason earnestly with a person for purposes of dissuasion or remonstrance.

g. to eliminate or make indistinct by or as if by wearing away a surface.

VOCABULARY 2. Use each word in a sentence of your own construction

1. Specimen –
   Your Sentence:

2. Subterfuge –
   Your Sentence:

3. Deformity –
   Your Sentence:

4. Impugn –
   Your Sentence:

5. Effaced –
   Your Sentence:

6. Heterogeneous –
   Your Sentence:

7. Expostulate–
   Your Sentence:

The Institutes of the Christian Religion — Book 1, Chapter 15, Worksheet 2 — Name

STUDY QUESTIONS

1. What is Calvin's main concern in the first paragraph?

2. What proves that man has a soul?

3. How does God's remedy for sin show that man was created in the image of God?

4. What are the "two parts" of the soul? In Adam, were both parts of his soul created good?

The Institutes of the Christian Religion — Book 1, Chapter 16, Worksheet 1 — Name

VOCABULARY 1. Match the word with the correct definition

1. Subjoin
2. Sophist
3. Feign
4. Influx
5. Aliment
6. Obloquy
7. Prescience
8. Interpose
9. Promiscuous
10. Abettors
11. Fortuitously

a. knowledge of things before they exist or happen; foreknowledge; foresight.
b. happening or produced by chance; accidental.
c. that which sustains; means of support.
d. casual; irregular; haphazard.
e. to place in an intervening position.
f. a captious or fallacious reasoner.
g. a strongly condemnatory utterance: abusive language.
h. to place in sequence or juxtaposition to something else.
i. the act of flowing in: a coming in.
j. to give fictional representation to.
k. a person who assists or supports (someone) in the achievement of a purpose.

VOCABULARY 2. Use each word in a sentence of your own construction

1. Subjoin –
   Your Sentence:

2. Sophist –
   Your Sentence:

3. Feign –
   Your Sentence:

Great Christian Classics: Four Essential Works of the Faith 143

4. Influx –
   Your Sentence:

5. Aliment –
   Your Sentence:

6. Obloquy –
   Your Sentence:

7. Prescience –
   Your Sentence:

8. Interpose –
   Your Sentence:

9. Promiscuous –
   Your Sentence:

10. Abettors –
    Your Sentence:

11. Fortuitously –
    Your Sentence:

The Institutes of the Christian Religion

| Book 1 Chapter 16 Worksheet 2 | Name |

Study Questions

1. What is providence? How is it different from, but related to God being the Creator?

2. For Calvin, does God's omnipotence mean that God is able to do anything? If not, what does he mean by omnipotence?

3. How would Calvin respond to the scientist who says, "God created the world, and He created laws like gravity, but God doesn't actually cause this heavy object to fall to the ground when I let go—nature does that."

4. How would Calvin respond to the preacher who says, "God has the power to intervene in nature and perform miracles, or He can choose to let nature take its course."

5. What is the difference between general (or universal) providence and special providence? What is Calvin's opinion of each?

6. What is wrong with saying that some things happen by chance?

The Institutes of the Christian Religion | Book 1 Chapter 17 Worksheet 1 | Name

VOCABULARY 1. Match the word with the correct definition

1. Subtlety
2. Paternal
3. Torpor
4. Advert
5. Inure
6. Provident
7. Petulantly
8. Puerilities
9. Temerity

a. reckless boldness; rashness.
b. to accustom to accept something undesirable.
c. fine or delicate in meaning or intent; difficult to perceive or understand.
d. having or showing foresight; providing carefully for the future.
e. moved to or showing sudden, impatient irritation, especially over some trifling annoyance.
f. characteristic of or befitting a father; fatherly.
g. childishly foolish; immature or trivial.
h. to turn the mind or attention.
i. a state of mental and motor inactivity with partial or total insensibility.

VOCABULARY 2. Use each word in a sentence of your own construction

1. Subtlety –
   Your Sentence:

2. Paternal –
   Your Sentence:

3. Torpor –
   Your Sentence:

4. Advert –
   Your Sentence:

Great Christian Classics: Four Essential Works of the Faith   147

5. Inure –
   Your Sentence:

6. Provident –
   Your Sentence:

7. Petulantly –
   Your Sentence:

8. Puerilities –
   Your Sentence:

9. Temerity –
   Your Sentence:

The Institutes of the Christian Religion — Book 1, Chapter 17, Worksheet 2

STUDY QUESTIONS

1. Describe two ways to abuse the belief in God's providence.

2. How did Solomon reconcile human deliberation with divine providence?

3. What are "lesser causes," and how should the Christian treat them?

4. What is the effect in the believer's heart of understanding what God has revealed about His providence?

5. What is your reaction to Calvin when he writes, "...the devil and all the ungodly are reined in by God, so that they cannot conceive, plan or carry out any crime, unless God allows it, indeed commands it."

The Institutes of the Christian Religion | Book 2 Chapter 1 Worksheet 1 | Name

VOCABULARY 1. Match the word with the correct definition

1. Primeval
2. Perdition
3. Depravity
4. Adduce
5. Contagion
6. Progenitor
7. Vitiated
8. Prolific
9. Pernicious
10. Imbued
11. Egregiously
12. Preposterously
13. Ignominy
14. Apportion
15. Arrogate
16. Indispose
17. Innate
18. Devoid
19. Plausible
20. Credulous
21. Endowments

a. to distribute or allocate proportionally; divide and assign according to some rule of proportional distribution.
b. being without a usual, typical, or expected attribute or accompaniment.
c. willing to believe or trust too readily, especially without proper or adequate evidence; gullible.
d. existing in one from birth; inborn; native.
e. to impair the quality of; make faulty; spoil.
f. to offer as an example, reason, or proof in a discussion or analysis.
g. producing in large quantities or with great frequency; highly productive.
h. marked by corruption or evil.
i. of or relating to the first age or ages, especially of the world.
j. extraordinary in some bad way; glaring; flagrant.
k. to make unfit.
l. disgraceful or dishonorable conduct, quality, or action.
m. to claim unwarrantably or presumptuously; assume or appropriate to oneself without right.
n. causing insidious harm or ruin; ruinous; injurious; hurtful.
o. completely contrary to nature, reason, or commom sense; absurd; senseless; utterly foolish.
p. to impregnate or inspire, as with feelings, opinions, etc.
q. eternal damnation.
r. the communication of disease by direct or indirect contact.
s. a biologically ancestral form.
t. to provide a permanent fund or source of income.
u. having an appearance of truth or reason; seemingly worthy of approval or acceptance; credible; believable.

VOCABULARY 2. Use each word in a sentence of your own construction

1. Primeval –
   Your Sentence:

2. Perdition –
   Your Sentence:

3. Depravity –
   Your Sentence:

4. Adduce –
   Your Sentence:

5. Contagion –
   Your Sentence:

6. Progenitor –
   Your Sentence:

7. Vitiated –
   Your Sentence:

8. Prolific –
   Your Sentence:

9. Pernicious –
   Your Sentence:

10. Imbued –
    Your Sentence:

11. Egregiously –
    Your Sentence:

12. Preposterously –
    Your Sentence:

13. Ignominy –
    Your Sentence:

14. Apportion –
    Your Sentence:

15. Arrogate –
    Your Sentence:

16. Indispose –
    Your Sentence:

17. Innate –
    Your Sentence:

18. Devoid –
    Your Sentence:

19. Plausible –
    Your Sentence:

20. Credulous –
    Your Sentence:

21. Endowments –
    Your Sentence:

The Institutes of the Christian Religion

Book 2
Chapter 1
Worksheet 2

Name

Study Questions

1. Which philosopher is credited with the proverb "know thyself"?

2. When Calvin says we should know ourselves, how is that different from the philosophers? According to Calvin, what are the two basic aspects of self-knowledge?

3. What does a Pelagian believe?

4. Why does Calvin insist that Adam's sin was not merely passed on to us by imitation of a bad example but by a real connection between Adam and us? How does this effect our view of Christ's work for us?

5. What does Calvin mean when he says, "Sins are the fruits of sin"? What is original sin?

The Institutes of the Christian Religion — Book 2, Chapter 2, Worksheet 1 — Name

VOCABULARY 1. Match the word with the correct definition

1. Grievous
2. Enumerate
3. Monstrous
4. Apposite
5. Adventitious
6. Antecedently

a. suitable; well-adapted; pertinent; relevant; apt.
b. burdensome or oppressive.
c. to ascertain the number of.
d. coming from another source and not inherent or innate.
e. a preceding circumstance, event, object, style, phenomenon, etc.
f. having extraordinary often overwhelming size.

VOCABULARY 2. Use each word in a sentence of your own construction

1. Grievous –
   Your Sentence:

2. Enumerate –
   Your Sentence:

3. Monstrous –
   Your Sentence:

4. Apposite –
   Your Sentence:

5. Adventitious –
   Your Sentence:

6. Antecedently –
   Your Sentence:

The Institutes of the Christian Religion

Book 2
Chapter 2
Worksheet 2

Name

Study Questions

1. What are man's natural gifts? What are his supernatural gifts?

2. Augustine said that the supernatural gifts were withdrawn from man at his fall and he still has the natural gifts though they are corrupted by sin. How are these gifts corrupted?

The Institutes of the Christian Religion | Book 2 Chapter 3 Worksheet 1 | Name

VOCABULARY 1. Match the word with the correct definition

1. Rapine
2. Cloister
3. Brocard
4. Rectitude
5. Evince
6. Conductive
7. Specious
8. Incontrovertible
9. Impetuously
10. Sophists
11. Invidious
12. Penury

a. not open to question or dispute; indisputable.
b. the quality or state of being correct in judgment or procedure.
c. a captious or fallacious reasoner.
d. the violent seizure and carrying off of another's property; plunder.
e. pleasing to the eye but deceptive.
f. of, relating to or characterized by sudden or rash action, emotion, etc.; impulsive.
g. extreme poverty; destitution.
h. having the property or capability of conducting.
i. to show clearly; make evident or manifest; prove.
j. offensively or unfairly discriminating; injurious.
k. an elementary principle or maxim: a short proverbial rule (as in law, ethics, or metaphysics).
l. a place of religious seclusion, as a monastery or convent.

VOCABULARY 2. Use each word in a sentence of your own construction

1. Rapine –
   Your Sentence:

2. Cloister –
   Your Sentence:

3. Brocard –
   Your Sentence:

4. Rectitude –
   Your Sentence:

5. Evince –
   Your Sentence:

6. Conductive –
   Your Sentence:

7. Specious –
   Your Sentence:

8. Incontrovertible –
   Your Sentence:

9. Impetuously –
   Your Sentence:

10. Sophists –
    Your Sentence:

11. Invidious –
    Your Sentence:

12. Penury –
    Your Sentence:

The Institutes of the Christian Religion | Book 2 Chapter 3 Worksheet 2 | Name

Study Questions

1. What is the difference between Cataline and Camillus, by human reckoning? What is the difference between the men from God's reckoning?

2. In what sense does man sin freely? In what sense is man bound to sin? What does Bernard mean by "voluntary bondage"?

3. How does God begin a good work in us?

4. What is Calvin's motivation for insisting that everything good in man's will was given to him by God?

5. Calvin uses the word "efficaciously." Use this word in a sentence summarizing the main point of this section.

The Institutes of the Christian Religion | Book 2 Chapter 6 Worksheet 1 | Name

VOCABULARY 1. Match the word with the correct definition

1. Piety
2. Malediction
3. Promulgation

a. to set forth or teach publicly.
b. a curse; imprecation.
c. reverence for God or devout fulfillment of religious obligations.

VOCABULARY 2. Use each word in a sentence of your own construction

1. Piety –
   Your Sentence:

2. Malediction –
   Your Sentence:

3. Promulgation –
   Your Sentence:

The Institutes of the Christian Religion

Book 2
Chapter 6
Worksheet 2

Name

Study Questions

1. "Although God graciously shows his fatherly goodness to us in many ways, we cannot infer he is a Father simply by looking at the world." What is required in order to see God as your Father?

The Institutes of the Christian Religion | Book 2 Chapter 7 Worksheet 1 | Name

VOCABULARY 1. Match the word with the correct definition

1. Exhort
2. Tribunal
3. Factitious
4. Execrate
5. Eulogium
6. Inexorable
7. Petulantly
8. Preclude
9. Denunciations
10. Certiorate
11. Derogate

a. warning of impending evil; threat.
b. moved to or showing sudden, impatient irritation, especially over some trifling annoyance.
c. certify, apprise, assure.
d. to prevent the presence, existence, or occurrence of; make impossible.
e. not spontaneous or natural; artificial; contrived.
f. high praise.
g. not to be persuaded, moved, or stopped.
h. to detract, as from authority, estimation.
i. utterly detestable; abominable; abhorrent.
j. a place or seat of judgment.
k. to incite by argument or advice: urge strongly.

VOCABULARY 2. Use each word in a sentence of your own construction

1. Exhort –
    Your Sentence:

2. Tribunal –
    Your Sentence:

3. Factitious –
    Your Sentence:

4. Execrate –

164 Great Christian Classics: Four Essential Works of the Faith

Your Sentence:

5. Eulogium –
   Your Sentence:

6. Inexorable –
   Your Sentence:

7. Petulantly –
   Your Sentence:

8. Preclude –
   Your Sentence:

9. Denunciations –
   Your Sentence:

10. Certiorate –
    Your Sentence:

11. Derogate –
    Your Sentence:

The Institutes of the Christian Religion

Book 2
Chapter 7
Worksheet 2

Name _____

Study Questions

1. What are the three uses of the Law?

2. Which of the three uses of the Law does Calvin say is the primary use? Why do you think Calvin says this is primary?

The Institutes of the Christian Religion — Book 2, Chapter 8, Worksheet 1

Name

VOCABULARY 1. Match the word with the correct definition

1. Abasement
2. Lethargy
3. Null
4. Imbue
5. Immured
6. Trepidation
7. Enumerate
8. Blandishments
9. Incurred
10. Animus

a. something that tends to coax or cajole.
b. to impregnate or inspire, as with feelings, opinions, etc.
c. the quality or state of being drowsy and dull, listless and unenergetic, or indifferent and lazy; apathetic or sluggish inactivity.
d. amounting to nothing.
e. to ascertain the number of.
f. to shut in; seclude or confine.
g. a nervous or fearful feeling of uncertain agitation.
h. to become liable or subject to through one's own action; bring or take upon oneself.
i. strong dislike or enmity; hostile attitude; animosity.
j. to reduce or lower, as in a rank, office, reputation, or estimation; humble; degrade.

VOCABULARY 2. Use each word in a sentence of your own construction

1. Abasement –
   Your Sentence:

2. Lethargy –
   Your Sentence:

3. Null –
   Your Sentence:

4. Imbue –
   Your Sentence:

5. Immured –
   Your Sentence:

6. Trepidation –
   Your Sentence:

7. Enumerate –
   Your Sentence:

8. Blandishments –
   Your Sentence:

9. Incurred –
   Your Sentence:

10. Animus –
    Your Sentence:

The Institutes of the Christian Religion — Book 2, Chapter 8, Worksheet 2 — Name

STUDY QUESTIONS

1. "The Lord is not satisfied with merely inspiring respect for his justice." With what is He satisfied with?

2. Does obedience to God deserve a reward? Why or why not?

3. How is God's Law different from the laws of men?

4. Compare the summaries of the Law given in Deuteronomy 10:12-13 and Luke 10:27.

The Institutes of the Christian Religion — Book 2, Chapter 9, Worksheet 1 — Name

VOCABULARY 1. Match the word with the correct definition

1. Consign
2. Gratuitous
3. Imputation
4. Rudiment

a. given, done, bestowed, or obtained without charge or payment; free.
b. an attribution, as of fault or crime; accusation.
c. a basic principle or element or a fundamental skill.
d. to banish or set apart in one's mind; relegate.

VOCABULARY 2. Use each word in a sentence of your own construction

1. Consign –
   Your Sentence:

2. Gratuitous –
   Your Sentence:

3. Imputation –
   Your Sentence:

4. Rudiment –
   Your Sentence:

Study Questions

1. In what ways are the Law and the Gospel in opposition?

2. In what way does Calvin say that the Gospel has not succeeded the Law?

3. How does Calvin conclude that the Gospel and Law differ?

The Institutes of the Christian Religion — Book 2, Chapter 12, Worksheet 1 — Name

VOCABULARY 1. Match the word with the correct definition

1. Subvert
2. Expiation
3. Injurious

a. the means by which atonement or reparation is made.
b. to undermine the principles of; pervert; corrupt.
c. harmful, hurtful, or detrimental, as in effect.

VOCABULARY 2. Use each word in a sentence of your own construction

1. Subvert –
   Your Sentence:

2. Expiation –
   Your Sentence:

3. Injurious –
   Your Sentence:

The Institutes of the Christian Religion — Book 2, Chapter 12, Worksheet 2 — Name

STUDY QUESTIONS

1. Why is it important that Christ is a man?

2. Why is it important that Christ is God?

The Institutes of the Christian Religion — Book 2, Chapter 14, Worksheet 1 — Name

VOCABULARY 1. Match the word with the correct definition

1. Similitude
2. Analogous
3. Absurdity
4. Conjured

a. similar or comparable to something else either in general or in some specific detail.
b. to affect or influence by or as if by invocation or spell.
c. likeness; resemblance.
d. utterly or obviously senseless, illogical, or untrue; contrary to all reason or common sense; laughably foolish or false.

VOCABULARY 2. Use each word in a sentence of your own construction

1. Similitude –
   Your Sentence:

2. Analogous –
   Your Sentence:

3. Absurdity –
   Your Sentence:

4. Conjured –
   Your Sentence:

Great Christian Classics: Four Essential Works of the Faith

The Institutes of the Christian Religion

Book 2
Chapter 14
Worksheet 2

Name

Study Questions

1. Is Calvin saying that Christ has a human body and a divine soul? What is the point of his illustration?

The Institutes of the Christian Religion | Book 2 Chapter 16 Worksheet 1 | Name

VOCABULARY 1. Match the word with the correct definition

1. Condiment
2. Enmity
3. Calamitous
4. Propitiation
5. Immemorial
6. Ineffable
7. Synecdoche
8. Insipid
9. Eschew
10. Ablution
11. Expiation
12. Ignoble
13. Ignominy
14. Archetype
15. Vacillating

a. a figure of speech in which a part is used for the whole or the whole for a part, the special for the general or the general for the special.
b. disgraceful or dishonorable conduct, quality, or action.
c. cleansing with water or other liquid.
d. to abstain or keep away from; shun; avoid.
e. being, causing, or accompanied by calamity.
f. the means by which atonement or reparation is made.
g. extending or existing since beyond the reach of memory, record, or tradition.
h. a pungent seasoning.
i. the act of gaining or regaining the favor or goodwill of someone or something.
j. a feeling or condition of hostility; hatred; ill will; animosity; antagonism.
k. incapable of being expressed or described in words.
l. not resolute; wavering; indecisive; hesitating.
m. the original pattern or model from which all things of the same kind are copied or on which they are based; a model or first form; prototype.
n. characterized by baseness, lowness, or meanness.
o. without distinctive, interesting, or stimulating qualities; vapid.

VOCABULARY 2. Use each word in a sentence of your own construction

1. Condiment –
   Your Sentence:

2. Enmity –
   Your Sentence:

3. Calamitous –
   Your Sentence:

4. Propitiation –
   Your Sentence:

5. Immemorial –
   Your Sentence:

6. Ineffable –
   Your Sentence:

7. Synecdoche –
   Your Sentence:

8. Insipid –
   Your Sentence:

9. Eschew –
   Your Sentence:

10. Ablution –
    Your Sentence:

11. Expiation –
    Your Sentence:

12. Ignoble –
    Your Sentence:

13. Ignominy –
    Your Sentence:

14. Archetype –
    Your Sentence:

15. Vacillating –
    Your Sentence:

The Institutes of the Christian Religion — Book 2, Chapter 16, Worksheet 2 — Name

STUDY QUESTIONS

1. Why must we recognize that we were God's enemies before being reconciled in Christ?

2. Why did Christ have to die on a cross rather than, say, at the hands of a lone assassin?

3. If Christ wiped out our sin and death with His death on the cross, why is it important that He rose again?

4. What began with Christ's ascension?

5. What is Christ doing while seated at the right hand of God the Father?

6. Does Christ have a human body in heaven?

7. What is Calvin's comfort when he thinks of the judgment day?

The Institutes of the Christian Religion

Book 3
Chapter 1
Worksheet 1

Name

VOCABULARY 1. Match the word with the correct definition

1. Engrafted
2. Unction

a. something used for anointing.
b. to insert into another.

VOCABULARY 2. Use each word in a sentence of your own construction

1. Engrafted –
   Your Sentence:

2. Unction –
   Your Sentence:

The Institutes of the Christian Religion — Book 3, Chapter 1, Worksheet 2 — Name

STUDY QUESTIONS

1. Who benefits from Christ's death and resurrection?

2. What is the role of the Spirit in our salvation?

The Institutes of the Christian Religion | Book 3 Chapter 2 Worksheet 1 | Name

VOCABULARY 1. Match the word with the correct definition

1. Dubious
2. Inviolable
3. Fickle
4. Serene
5. Engrossed
6. Adjudge
7. Tumultuous
8. Perturbation

a. highly agitated, as the mind or emotions; distraught; turbulent.
b. doubtful; marked by or occasioning doubt.
c. to occupy completely, as the mind or attention; absorb.
d. marked by lack of steadfastness, constancy, or stability: given to erratic changeableness.
e. prohibiting violation; secure from destruction, violence, infringement, or desecration.
f. shining bright and steady.
g. great disturbance or disquieting in mind.
h. to declare or pronounce formally; decree.

VOCABULARY 2. Use each word in a sentence of your own construction

1. Dubious –
   Your Sentence:

2. Inviolable –
   Your Sentence:

3. Fickle –
   Your Sentence:

4. Serene –
   Your Sentence:

5. Engrossed –
   Your Sentence:

6. Adjudge –
   Your Sentence:

7. Tumultuous –
   Your Sentence:

8. Perturbation –
   Your Sentence:

Study Questions

1. What is the "object" of faith?

2. What is the relationship between faith and the Word (or faith and doctrine)?

3. What is Calvin's "complete definition of faith"? Note that it is a Trinitarian definition.

4. Is assurance and confidence in our salvation a necessary part of having faith? Will we ever be completely free of distrust?

The Institutes of the Christian Religion — Book 3, Chapter 3, Worksheet 1 — Name

VOCABULARY 1. Match the word with the correct definition

1. Repentance
2. Disposition
3. Mortification
4. Averse
5. Neophyte

a. having a strong feeling of opposition, antipathy, repugnance, etc.; opposed.
b. deep sorrow, compunction, or contrition for a past sin, wrongdoing, or the like.
c. a new convert.
d. a sense of humiliation and shame caused by something that wounds one's pride or self-respect.
e. physical inclination or tendency.

VOCABULARY 2. Use each word in a sentence of your own construction

1. Repentance –
   Your Sentence:

2. Disposition –
   Your Sentence:

3. Mortification –
   Your Sentence:

4. Averse –
   Your Sentence:

5. Neophyte –
   Your Sentence:

The Institutes of the Christian Religion — Book 3, Chapter 3, Worksheet 2

STUDY QUESTIONS

1. Is a truly holy life essential to salvation? If so, does this contradict what Calvin has said about justification being free and by faith alone? Why not?

2. Describe in your own words what it means to mortify the flesh.

3. What happens to a person's sin when they are born again? What remains to be done to their sin for the rest of their life?

The Institutes of the Christian Religion — Book 3 Chapter 6 Worksheet 1 — Name

VOCABULARY 1. Match the word with the correct definition

1. Volubility
2. Loquacious
3. Sophistry
4. Alacrity
5. Eloquence

a. the practice or art of using language with fluency and aptness.
b. captious or fallacious reasoning.
c. characterized by a ready and continuous flow of words; fluent; glib.
d. characterized by excessive talk; wordy.
e. cheerful readiness, promptness, or willingness.

VOCABULARY 2. Use each word in a sentence of your own construction

1. Volubility –
   Your Sentence:

2. Loquacious –
   Your Sentence:

3. Sophistry –
   Your Sentence:

4. Alacrity –
   Your Sentence:

5. Eloquence –
   Your Sentence:

The Institutes of the Christian Religion — Book 3, Chapter 6, Worksheet 2

Study Questions

1. Calvin says "...no one can have fellowship with Christ, unless they have acquired genuine knowledge of him from the Gospel." Explain what Calvin means by "knowledge" in this context.

2. How can doctrine be a matter of life as Calvin says? Can't a person learn theology without being a disciple of Christ?

The Institutes of the Christian Religion | Book 3 Chapter 7 Worksheet 1 | Name

VOCABULARY 1. Match the word with the correct definition

1. Profane
2. Carnal
3. Proficiency
4. Minutest
5. Allure

a. advancement in knowledge or skill.
b. to attract or tempt by something flattering or desirable.
c. characterized by irreverence or contempt for God or sacred principles or things; irreligious.
d. not spiritual; merely human; temporal; worldly.
e. very small.

VOCABULARY 2. Use each word in a sentence of your own construction

1. Profane –
   Your Sentence:

2. Carnal –
   Your Sentence:

3. Proficiency –
   Your Sentence:

4. Minutest –
   Your Sentence:

5. Allure –
   Your Sentence:

The Institutes of the Christian Religion — Book 3, Chapter 7, Worksheet 2

Study Questions

1. What error was made by "the philosophers of old"?

2. When a believer denies his own desires and his own pride, what does he replace them with?

3. How does a believer's self-denial relate to the Church?

The Institutes of the Christian Religion — Book 3, Chapter 8, Worksheet 1 — Name

VOCABULARY 1. Match the word with the correct definition

1. Indulgently
2. Elated
3. Pious
4. Overweening
5. Refractory

a. to be conceited or arrogant.
b. willing to allow excessive leniency, generosity, or consideration.
c. very happy or proud; jubilant; in high spirits.
d. hard or impossible to manage; stubbornly disobedient.
e. having or showing a dutiful spirit of reverence for God.

VOCABULARY 2. Use each word in a sentence of your own construction

1. Indulgently –
   Your Sentence:

2. Elated –
   Your Sentence:

3. Pious –
   Your Sentence:

4. Overweening –
   Your Sentence:

5. Refractory –
   Your Sentence:

The Institutes of the Christian Religion — Book 3, Chapter 8, Worksheet 2

STUDY QUESTIONS

1. How does Calvin use the example of David in Psalm 30:6-7?

2. How can tribulation increase your faith?

3. Why are Christians not all given the same trials by God?

4. What are the two parts of a proper response to trials that come our way? Which should be the main part?

The Institutes of the Christian Religion — Book 3, Chapter 9, Worksheet 1 — Name

VOCABULARY 1. Match the word with the correct definition

1. Disencumber
2. Bereavement
3. Sterility
4. Dazzled
5. Admixture
6. Terrestrial
7. Benignity

a. to overpower or dim the vision of by intense light.
b. pertaining to, consisting of, or representing the earth as distinct from other planets.
c. to free from a burden or other encumbrance; disburden.
d. the act of mixing; state of being mixed.
e. showing kindness and gentleness.
f. a state of intense grief, as after the loss of a loved one; desolation.
g. not productive of results, ideas, etc.

VOCABULARY 2. Use each word in a sentence of your own construction

1. Disencumber –
   Your Sentence:

2. Bereavement –
   Your Sentence:

3. Sterility –
   Your Sentence:

4. Dazzled –
   Your Sentence:

5. Admixture –
   Your Sentence:

6. Terrestrial –
   Your Sentence:

7. Benignity –
   Your Sentence:

The Institutes of the Christian Religion

Book 3
Chapter 9
Worksheet 2

Name

Study Questions

1. Why should we "despise the world"?

2. How can a person sin by despising the world in the wrong way?

The Institutes of the Christian Religion — Book 3, Chapter 10, Worksheet 1   Name

VOCABULARY 1. Match the word with the correct definition

1. Shun
2. Fetters
3. Ostentation
4. Abstinence

a. anything that confines or restrains.
b. any self-restraint, self-denial, or forbearance.
c. to avoid deliberately and especially habitually.
d. characterized by or given to pretentious or conspicuous show in an attempt to impress others.

VOCABULARY 2. Use each word in a sentence of your own construction

1. Shun –
   Your Sentence:

2. Fetters –
   Your Sentence:

3. Ostentation –
   Your Sentence:

4. Abstinence –
   Your Sentence:

The Institutes of the Christian Religion

Book 3
Chapter 10
Worksheet 2

Name

Study Questions

1. What is Calvin's principle for how we are to use God's gifts?

2. What does it tell you about God that He didn't just make food nutritious but that He made it taste good and made it in all its variety?

3. Is there a way to test to see if you are enjoying God's creation rightly?

The Institutes of the Christian Religion — Book 3, Chapter 11, Worksheet 1 — Name

VOCABULARY 1. Match the word with the correct definition

1. Justification
2. Remission
3. Attestation

a. to release from the guilt or penalty of.
b. an affirmation of something to be true or genuine.
c. an acceptable reason for doing something: something that justifies an act or way of behaving.

VOCABULARY 2. Use each word in a sentence of your own construction

1. Justification –
   Your Sentence:

2. Remission –
   Your Sentence:

3. Attestation –
   Your Sentence:

The Institutes of the Christian Religion

Book 3
Chapter 11
Worksheet 2

Name

STUDY QUESTIONS

1. To be justified in the sight of God, must a person be considered righteous in the judgment of God? Explain.

2. Are we saved by faith, or are we saved by Christ? What is the difference?

3. What is the difference between obtaining righteousness by "imputation" and by "influence"?

The Institutes of the Christian Religion — Book 3, Chapter 12, Worksheet 1 — Name

VOCABULARY 1. Match the word with the correct definition

1. Presumption
2. Precinct
3. Logomachy

a. a dispute over or about words.
b. an enclosure bounded by the walls of a building.
c. belief on reasonable grounds or probable evidence.

VOCABULARY 2. Use each word in a sentence of your own construction

1. Presumption –
   Your Sentence:

2. Precinct –
   Your Sentence:

3. Logomachy –
   Your Sentence:

The Institutes of the Christian Religion

| Book 3 Chapter 12 Worksheet 2 | Name |

Study Questions

1. Relate this chapter to the subject of Book I, Chapter 1.

The Institutes of the Christian Religion | Book 3 Chapter 13 Worksheet 1 | Name

VOCABULARY 1. Match the word with the correct definition

1. Vacillate

2. Fluctuate

a. to change continually; shift back and forth; vary irregularly.

b. not resolute; wavering; indecisive; hesitating.

VOCABULARY 2. Use each word in a sentence of your own construction

1. Vacillate –
   Your Sentence:

2. Fluctuate –
   Your Sentence:

The Institutes of the Christian Religion

Book 3
Chapter 13
Worksheet 2

Name

Study Questions

1. Calvin says, "When it looks at God, the conscience must either be completely at peace or full of the terror of hell." Is there no neutral ground in our relationship to God? Why?

The Institutes of the Christian Religion — Book 3, Chapter 14, Worksheet 1   Name

VOCABULARY 1. Match the word with the correct definition

1. Sedition
2. Emulation
3. Contaminate
4. Vitiate
5. Integrity

a. ambition or endeavor to equal or excel others.
b. adherence to moral and ethical principles; soundness of moral character; honesty.
c. any action, especially in speech or writing, promoting such discontent or rebellion.
d. to soil, stain, corrupt, or infect by contact or association.
e. to impair the quality of; make faulty; spoil.

VOCABULARY 2. Use each word in a sentence of your own construction

1. Sedition –
   Your Sentence:

2. Emulation –
   Your Sentence:

3. Contaminate –
   Your Sentence:

4. Vitiate –
   Your Sentence:

5. Integrity –
   Your Sentence:

The Institutes of the Christian Religion — Book 3, Chapter 14, Worksheet 2

STUDY QUESTIONS

1. What is unrighteous about the "natural gifts," such as the sense of justice that can be shown by an unbeliever?

2. How are we to view our good works after justification? Are they now the basis of our standing before God? Should they encourage us? Why?

The Institutes of the Christian Religion

Book 3
Chapter 16
Worksheet 1

Name

VOCABULARY 1. Match the word with the correct definition

1. Calumnies

2. Zealot

3. Comprehend

a. the act of uttering false charges or misrepresentations maliciously calculated to harm another's reputation.

b. to understand the nature or meaning of; grasp with the mind; perceive.

c. an excessively zealous person; fanatic.

VOCABULARY 2. Use each word in a sentence of your own construction

1. Calumnies –
   Your Sentence:

2. Zealot –
   Your Sentence:

3. Comprehend –
   Your Sentence:

The Institutes of the Christian Religion — Book 3, Chapter 16, Worksheet 2 — Name

STUDY QUESTIONS

1. After preaching justification by faith, why is it that Calvin says we are not justified without works?

The Institutes of the Christian Religion — Book 3, Chapter 17, Worksheet 1

VOCABULARY 1. Match the word with the correct definition

1. Efface
2. Exempt
3. Approbation
4. Cognizance
5. Tribunal

a. awareness, realization, or knowledge; notice; perception.
b. to eliminate or make indistinct by or as if by wearing away a surface.
c. a place or seat of judgment.
d. to free from an obligation or liability to which others are subject; release.
e. approval; commendation.

VOCABULARY 2. Use each word in a sentence of your own construction

1. Effaced –
   Your Sentence:

2. Exempt –
   Your Sentence:

3. Approbation –
   Your Sentence:

4. Cognizance –
   Your Sentence:

5. Tribunal –
   Your Sentence:

| *The Institutes of the Christian Religion* | Book 3 Chapter 17 Worksheet 2 | Name |

Study Questions

1. We know that we can be justified (considered righteous) by being united to Christ. Can our imperfect works also be justified (considered righteous)? How?

The Institutes of the Christian Religion — Book 3, Chapter 18, Worksheet 1

VOCABULARY 1. Match the word with the correct definition

1. Aspiration
2. Inextricable
3. Genial
4. Profusion

a. incapable of being disentangled, undone, loosed, or solved.
b. abundance; abundant quantity.
c. a strong desire, longing, or aim; ambition.
d. favorable for life, growth, or comfort; pleasantly warm; comfortably mild.

VOCABULARY 2. Use each word in a sentence of your own construction

1. Aspiration –
   Your Sentence:

2. Inextricable –
   Your Sentence:

3. Genial –
   Your Sentence:

4. Profusion –
   Your Sentence:

The Institutes of the Christian Religion

Book 3
Chapter 18
Worksheet 2

Name _____

STUDY QUESTIONS

1. What are the three parts of Christian freedom, and how are each of them related to the three uses of the Law? Is one of the uses of the Law not related to Christian freedom?

The Institutes of the Christian Religion — Book 3, Chapter 20, Worksheet 1

VOCABULARY 1. Match the word with the correct definition

1. Implore

2. Levity

3. Ingenuous

4. Invoke

a. to call for with earnest desire; make supplication or pray for.

b. showing innocent or childlike simplicity and candidness.

c. the lightness of mind, character, or behavior; lack of appropriate seriousness or earnestness.

d. to beg urgently or piteously, as for aid or mercy; beseech; entreat.

VOCABULARY 2. Use each word in a sentence of your own construction

1. Implore –
   Your Sentence:

2. Levity –
   Your Sentence:

3. Ingenuous –
   Your Sentence:

4. Invoke –
   Your Sentence:

The Institutes of the Christian Religion

| Book 3　Chapter 20　Worksheet 2 | Name |

Study Questions

1. If God already knows what we need, why must we pray?

2. Calvin says that a praying believer needs to have both an awareness of need and a trust in God. How does the absence of each of these lead a person not to pray?

3. Of Calvin's four "rules" of prayer presented in this chapter, which is the one you need to improve on the most?

The Institutes of the Christian Religion — Book 3, Chapter 21, Worksheet 1 — Name

VOCABULARY 1. Match the word with the correct definition

1. Election
2. Promiscuous
3. Repugnant
4. Brutish

a. casual; irregular; haphazard.
b. brutal; cruel.
c. the choice by God of individuals, as for a particular work or for favor or salvation.
d. distasteful, objectionable, or offensive.

VOCABULARY 2. Use each word in a sentence of your own construction

1. Election –
   Your Sentence:

2. Promiscuous –
   Your Sentence:

3. Repugnant –
   Your Sentence:

4. Brutish –
   Your Sentence:

The Institutes of the Christian Religion — Book 3, Chapter 21, Worksheet 2

STUDY QUESTIONS

1. How does Calvin use Romans 11:5-6 to support the doctrine that God chooses a remnant of people for salvation? What other doctrine, of which he has previously written, does he use here as the basis of his argument for the doctrine of eternal election?

2. What is Calvin warning against in this chapter?

The Institutes of the Christian Religion — Book 3, Chapter 22, Worksheet 1

Name

VOCABULARY 1. Match the word with the correct definition

1. Vulgar
2. Candid
3. Petulance
4. Conciliate

a. marked by honest sincere expression.
b. insolent or rude in speech or behavior.
c. to win or gain.
d. morally crude, undeveloped, or unregenerate.

VOCABULARY 2. Use each word in a sentence of your own construction

1. Vulgar –
   Your Sentence:

2. Candid –
   Your Sentence:

3. Petulance –
   Your Sentence:

4. Conciliate –
   Your Sentence:

The Institutes of the Christian Religion — Book 3, Chapter 22, Worksheet 2 — Name

Study Questions

1. Why is it important to Calvin that God didn't just know in advance who will one day be saved, but that He actually chose who will be saved?

2. Calvin talks about God's freedom in this chapter. Why do you think we hear more about man's freedom in our culture?

The Institutes of the Christian Religion | Book 3 Chapter 24 Worksheet 1 | Name

VOCABULARY 1. Match the word with the correct definition

1. Disquieting
2. Adhere
3. Repress

4. Dissuade
5. Tranquil

6. Infatuated

a. to advise (a person) against something.
b. causing anxiety or uneasiness; disturbing.
c. to inspire or possess with a foolish or unreasoning passion.
d. to keep under control, check, or suppress.
e. to be devoted in support or allegiance; be attached as a follower or upholder.
f. free from commotion or tumult; peaceful; quiet; calm.

VOCABULARY 2. Use each word in a sentence of your own construction

1. Disquieting –
   Your Sentence:

2. Adhere –
   Your Sentence:

3. Repress –
   Your Sentence:

4. Dissuade –
   Your Sentence:

5. Tranquil –
   Your Sentence:

6. Infatuated –
   Your Sentence:

Study Questions

1. How can we be assured that we are saved? What is Calvin's answer?

2. How can we be confident that we will not fall away from the faith in the future?

The Institutes of the Christian Religion

**Book 3
Chapter 25
Worksheet 1**

Name

VOCABULARY 1. Match the word with the correct definition

1. Surmount
2. Auxiliary
3. Appertain
4. Dissevered

a. to belong as a part, right, possession, attribute, etc.; pertain or relate.
b. to mount upon; get on the top of; mount upon and cross over.
c. to part; separate.
d. additional; supplementary; reserve.

VOCABULARY 2. Use each word in a sentence of your own construction

1. Surmount –
   Your Sentence:

2. Auxiliary –
   Your Sentence:

3. Appertain –
   Your Sentence:

4. Dissevered –
   Your Sentence:

The Institutes of the Christian Religion — Book 3, Chapter 25, Worksheet 2

STUDY QUESTIONS

1. How do you know your body will be resurrected from the dead?

The Institutes of the Christian Religion — Book 4, Chapter 1, Worksheet 1 — Name

VOCABULARY 1. Match the word with the correct definition

1. Consummation
2. Papacy
3. Avaricious
4. Sacrilegious
5. Schism
6. Incur
7. Moroseness
8. Patronize
9. Connivance
10. Machinations

a. to behave in an offensively condescending manner toward.
b. the violation or profanation of anything sacred or held sacred.
c. to bring to a state of perfection; fulfill.
d. characterized by avarice; greedy; covetous.
e. the office, dignity, or jurisdiction of the pope.
f. to contrive or plot, especially artfully or with evil purpose.
g. having a sullen and gloomy disposition.
h. to pretend ignorance of or fail to take action against something one ought to oppose.
i. formal division in or separation from a church.
j. to become liable or subject to. Bring down upon oneself.

VOCABULARY 2. Use each word in a sentence of your own construction

1. Consummation –
   Your Sentence:

2. Papacy –
   Your Sentence:

3. Avaricious –
   Your Sentence:

4. Sacrilegious –
   Your Sentence:

Great Christian Classics: Four Essential Works of the Faith   225

5. Schism –
   Your Sentence:

6. Incur –
   Your Sentence:

7. Moroseness –
   Your Sentence:

8. Patronize –
   Your Sentence:

9. Connivance –
   Your Sentence:

10. Machinations –
    Your Sentence:

The Institutes of the Christian Religion — Book 4, Chapter 1, Worksheet 2 — Name

Study Questions

1. Calvin uses two different analogies to talk about the Church: he calls the Church "Israel," and he calls it "your mother." What do these analogies say about the Church?

2. Can evil hypocrites be Church members? What are the two possible reasons why a hypocrite is not removed from the Church?

3. What is the "loving assessment" and how does this relate to the quote from Augustine in the same section? Finally, what does Calvin say is more essential than knowing if someone else in the Church is really saved?

4. The visible Church is visible, but what does it look like? How do you know it when you see it?

5. How can Calvin say "revolt from the Church is a denial of God and Christ?"

6. What is an example of a good reason to leave a church? What is an example of a poor reason to leave a church?

The Institutes of the Christian Religion | Book 4 Chapter 2 Worksheet 1 | Name

VOCABULARY 1. Match the word with the correct definition

1. Ensue
2. Bishop
3. Pretense
4. Assertion
5. Frivolous
6. Ascendancy
7. Usurp

a. the state of being in the ascendant; governing or controlling influence; domination.
b. a false show of something.
c. to strive to attain: pursue.
d. characterized by lack of seriousness or sense.
e. to seize and hold by force or without legal right.
f. a positive statement or declaration, often without support or reason.
g. a spiritual supervisor, overseer, or the like.

VOCABULARY 2. Use each word in a sentence of your own construction

1. Ensue –
   Your Sentence:

2. Bishop –
   Your Sentence:

3. Pretense –
   Your Sentence:

4. Assertion –
   Your Sentence:

5. Frivolous –
   Your Sentence:

6. Ascendancy –
   Your Sentence:

7. Usurp –
   Your Sentence:

The Institutes of the Christian Religion

Book 4
Chapter 2
Worksheet 2

Name

Study Questions

1. After the previous chapter where Calvin warned of revolting against the Church, how does Calvin object to the Church of Rome?

2. Papists say that their church is the only true Church because it has apostolic succession—an unbroken line of bishops all the way back to the apostles. How does Calvin respond?

The Institutes of the Christian Religion — Book 4, Chapter 3, Worksheet 1

VOCABULARY 1. Match the word with the correct definition

1. Docility
2. Disparage
3. Eulogize
4. Fruition

a. to praise highly.
b. the attainment of anything desired; realization; accomplishment.
c. to bring reproach or discredit upon; lower the estimation of.
d. easily managed or handled; tractable.

VOCABULARY 2. Use each word in a sentence of your own construction

1. Docility –
   Your Sentence:

2. Disparage –
   Your Sentence:

3. Eulogize –
   Your Sentence:

4. Fruition –
   Your Sentence:

The Institutes of the Christian Religion

Book 4
Chapter 3
Worksheet 2

Name

Study Questions

1. Why does God use men to lead the Church (as opposed to angels or direct visions of Christ)? Calvin gives several reasons.

2. What gifts did Christ give the Church after His ascension into heaven?

The Institutes of the Christian Religion | Book 4 Chapter 12 Worksheet 1 | Name

VOCABULARY 1. Match the word with the correct definition

1. Jurisdiction
2. Delinquencies
3. Captious
4. Seditious
5. Promiscuous

a. any action, especially in speech or writing, promoting such discontent or rebellion.
b. apt to notice and make much of trivial faults or defects; faultfinding; difficult to please.
c. casual; irregular; haphazard.
d. the power, right, or authority to interpret and apply the law.
e. failure in or neglect of duty or obligation; dereliction; default.

VOCABULARY 2. Use each word in a sentence of your own construction

1. Jurisdiction –
   Your Sentence:

2. Delinquencies –
   Your Sentence:

3. Captious –
   Your Sentence:

4. Seditious –
   Your Sentence:

5. Promiscuous –
   Your Sentence:

The Institutes of the Christian Religion — Book 4, Chapter 12, Worksheet 2

STUDY QUESTIONS

1. What four degrees of Church discipline does Calvin list, and where does he find them in the Bible?

2. What are the three reasons given why the Church must exercise discipline?

The Institutes of the Christian Religion — Book 4, Chapter 14, Worksheet 1 — Name

VOCABULARY 1. Match the word with the correct definition

1. Antecedent
2. Appertaining
3. Propitious
4. Efficacy
5. Instrumentality

a. the fact or function of serving some purpose.
b. presenting favorable conditions; favorable.
c. a preceding circumstance, event, object, style, phenomenon, etc.
d. to belong as a part, right, possession, attribute, etc.; pertain or relate.
e. capacity for producing a desired result or effect; effectiveness.

VOCABULARY 2. Use each word in a sentence of your own construction

1. Antecedent –
   Your Sentence:

2. Appertaining –
   Your Sentence:

3. Propitious –
   Your Sentence:

4. Efficacy –
   Your Sentence:

5. Instrumentality –
   Your Sentence:

The Institutes of the Christian Religion — Book 4, Chapter 14, Worksheet 2

STUDY QUESTIONS

1. How are the sacraments signs? What are they signs of?

2. How are sacraments seals and not merely a presentation of information?

The Institutes of the Christian Religion

Book 4
Chapter 15
Worksheet 1

Name

VOCABULARY 1. Match the word with the correct definition

1. Initiatory
2. Hallucination
3. Engrafted
4. Inveigh
5. Impunity

a. to insert into another.
b. exemption from punishment.
c. introductory; initial.
d. a false notion, belief, or impression; illusion; delusion.
e. to protest strongly or attack vehemently with words; rail.

VOCABULARY 2. Use each word in a sentence of your own construction

1. Initiatory –
   Your Sentence:

2. Hallucination –
   Your Sentence:

3. Engrafted –
   Your Sentence:

4. Inveigh –
   Your Sentence:

5. Impunity –
   Your Sentence:

The Institutes of the Christian Religion — Book 4, Chapter 15, Worksheet 2 — Name

STUDY QUESTIONS

1. What are the three benefits of baptism Calvin gives in this chapter?

2. In the previous chapter, Calvin said, "Nor should our confidence be attached to the sacraments..." Yet in this chapter, he exhorts us several times to remember our baptism. To what end should we do this, and how does that not constitute putting our confidence in baptism?

The Institutes of the Christian Religion | Book 4 Chapter 16 Worksheet 1 | Name

VOCABULARY 1. Match the word with the correct definition

1. Appendage
2. Consolation
3. Fallacious
4. Subordinate
5. Abrogate
6. Redound
7. Adjuration

a. to put aside; put an end to.
b. an earnest request; entreaty.
c. to alleviate or lessen the grief, sorrow, or disappointment of; give solace or comfort.
d. to have a good or bad effect or result, as to the advantage or disadvantage of a person or thing.
e. placed in or belonging to a lower order or rank.
f. deceptive; misleading.
g. a subordinate part attached to something; an auxiliary part; addition.

VOCABULARY 2. Use each word in a sentence of your own construction

1. Appendage –
   Your Sentence:

2. Consolation –
   Your Sentence:

3. Fallacious –
   Your Sentence:

4. Subordinate –
   Your Sentence:

5. Abrogate –
   Your Sentence:

6. Redound –
   Your Sentence:

7. Adjuration –
   Your Sentence:

The Institutes of the Christian Religion

Book 4
Chapter 16
Worksheet 2

Name

Study Questions

1. What are the promises signified by circumcision that God offered the people of God? Are these the same or different promises as those signified by baptism?

2. What is Calvin's argument for baptizing infants in the Church?

The Institutes of the Christian Religion — Book 4, Chapter 17, Worksheet 1 — Name

VOCABULARY 1. Match the word with the correct definition

1. Provident
2. Immortality
3. Exhilarate
4. Corporeal

a. to enliven; invigorate; stimulate.
b. having or showing foresight; providing carefully for the future.
c. of the nature of the physical body; bodily.
d. immortal condition or quality; unending life.

VOCABULARY 2. Use each word in a sentence of your own construction

1. Provident –
   Your Sentence:

2. Immortality –
   Your Sentence:

3. Exhilarate –
   Your Sentence:

4. Corporeal –
   Your Sentence:

The Institutes of the Christian Religion — Book 4, Chapter 17, Worksheet 2 — Name

STUDY QUESTIONS

1. What is the chief object of the Lord's Supper?

2. Explain why the Lord's Supper is not an empty sign.

The Institutes of the Christian Religion — Essay — Name

ESSAY ASSIGNMENT Provide a 500-word essay on **one** of the following subject areas.

1. What is Calvin's view of the relationship between the Law and the Gospel? What does freedom mean for a Christian?

2. Compare and contrast Calvin's view of predestination with that of Augustine. Do they both believe in predestination— God's sovereignty over man's salvation? Do they both believe there are men predestined to hell as well as to heaven (This belief is sometimes called "double predestination")?

3. Calvin has been called the "theologian of the Spirit." How is Calvin's view of the Holy Spirit (and the Trinity) important in order to understand the other major areas of his doctrine (for example, his views on Scripture, justification by faith, assurance, the Church, the sacraments, and the Christian life)?

4. Summarize Calvin's doctrine of man, including what it is to be created in the image of God and what are the effects of original sin.

5. What role do the ideas of gift and gratitude play in Calvin's thought?

6. Summarize Calvin's epistemology. What are the various sources of knowledge? What are the various topics of knowledge?

7. What role does the idea of union with Christ (in our salvation, in the Church as the body of Christ, and in the sacraments) play in Calvin's thought?

8. Write a fictional debate between someone who believes in Calvin's view of predestination and someone who believes men can decide if they want to be saved. Be sure to include Scripture in the debate.

9. Compare and contrast Calvin's view of the Lord's Supper to that of Luther and that of Zwingli.

| *The Institutes of the Christian Religion* | Exam | Scope: Calvin | Total score: ____ of 100 | Name |

MULTIPLE CHOICE Circle all that apply. (5 points each)

1. According to Calvin, what does true wisdom consist in?
    A. Knowledge of the Bible
    B. Faith in Christ
    C. Knowledge of God and Ourselves
    D. Obedience to God's commandments

2. Which ancient philosopher often said the proverb "know thyself"?
    A. Seneca
    B. Aristotle
    C. Plato
    D. Lucretius

3. What does Pelagianism teach?
    A. That man is born sinful and in need of God's grace and mercy
    B. That each person inherits a sinful nature from their parents
    C. That salvation comes through Christ alone
    D. That each person does not inherit a sinful nature from their parents

4. What theologian of the early church does Calvin most often quote from?
    A. Irenaeus
    B. Augustine
    C. John Chrysostom
    D. Origen

5. Which theologian of the Middle Ages does Calvin quote approvingly?
    A. Bernard of Clairvaux
    B. Thomas Aquinas
    C. Peter Abelard
    D. Peter Lombard

6. According to Calvin, what does man consist of?
    A. Body, Soul, and Spirit
    B. A living soul
    C. A physical body
    D. Body and Soul

7. Which of Calvin's "three uses of the law" is the primary use?
   A. First Use
   B. Second Use
   C. Third Use
   D. None of the above

8. According to Calvin, what is the orthodox doctrine of the person of Christ?
   A. Two natures in two persons
   B. One nature in two persons
   C. One nature in one person
   D. Two natures in one person

9. What does the message of the gospel consist in according to Calvin?
   A. Repentance and forgiveness of sins
   B. Faith and Love
   C. Christ's death on the cross
   D. God's mercy

10. How do we obtain the righteousness of Christ in justification?
    A. It is infused in us by the Spirit
    B. It is imputed to us by faith
    C. It is earned by good works
    D. It is received in baptism

11. What are the two parts of the soul according to Calvin?
    A. Heart and mind
    B. Mind and desire
    C. Intellect and will
    D. Free will and thought

12. What is the "sum of the Christian life" according to Calvin?
    A. Faith, hope, and love
    B. Faith in Jesus Christ
    C. Obedience to God's commandments
    D. Self-Denial

13. In what condition is man born, according to Calvin?

    A. Man is born with a partial corruption of sin from his parents

    B. Man is born totally depraved inheriting a sinful nature from his parents

    C. Man is born without sin but freely sins after birth

    D. Man is born unable to sin until the time of maturity

FILL IN THE BLANK

1. List the three uses of the law:_____
2. List the offices of Christ:_____
3. List Calvin's marks of a true church:_____

SHORT ANSWER

1. What is the doctrine of God's providence?

2. According to Calvin, what is the relationship between justification and sanctification?

3. Briefly summarize Calvin's argument for infant baptism.

4. How does Calvin summarize the moral law?

Match the Following

1. Pelagius

    a. Taught that man's supernatural gifts were withdrawn and natural gifts were corrupted by the fall.

2. Augustine

    b. Taught that reason was the sole ruler of man.

3. Greek Philosophers

    c. Taught that Rome is a true church since they maintain unbroken succession of bishops from the Apostles.

4. Papists

    d. Considered a noble and virtuous man by the Romans.

5. Camillus

    e. Taught that babies are not stained by original sin.

The Pilgrim's Progress — Book 1, Chapter 1, Worksheet 1 — Name

VOCABULARY 1. Match the word with the correct definition

1. Tophet
2. Pliable
3. Fantastical
4. Ravish
5. Odious

a. fanciful or capricious
b. to fill with strong emotion, especially joy
c. the place of punishment for the wicked after death; hell
d. highly offensive; repugnant; disgusting
e. easily influenced or persuaded

VOCABULARY 2. Use each word in a sentence of your own construction.

1. Tophet –
   Your Sentence:

2. Pliable –
   Your Sentence:

3. Fantastical –
   Your Sentence:

4. Ravish –
   Your Sentence:

5. Odious –

   Your Sentence:

The Pilgrim's Progress — Book 1, Chapter 1, Worksheet 2 — Name

Study Questions

1. What is an allegory, and how does this story fit the description of an allegory?

2. What were the motivations for the pilgrim to start upon his journey?

3. What is the biblical precedent for the instruction to fly from the City of Destruction?

4. What is the burden that Christian bears, and why is it that nobody else senses a burden?

5. Why was the rest of his family hesitant to join him in his journey? How does this compare with the families presented in the book of Acts?

6. How do Obstinate and Pliable represent two different ways people receive the warning to flee from the wrath that is to come?

7. How does Christian's reaction to the Slough of Despond differ from Pliable's response?

8. What is the substance of Mr. Worldly Wiseman's view of salvation? What sort of religions or denominations might teach this view?

9. Describe the Characters: What sort of character traits and what sort of people is Bunyan trying to describe by means of the characters he uses? In the case of the unbelievers allegorized, what sort of heresies might they believe?

a. Christian
b. Evangelist
c. Obstinate
d. Pliable
e. Help
f. Mr. Worldly Wiseman

The Pilgrim's Progress | Book 1 Chapter 2 Worksheet 1 | Name

VOCABULARY 1. Match the word with the correct definition

1. Vouchsafe

2. Slough

3. Betterment

4. Carnal

5. Indignation

a. strong displeasure at something considered unjust, offensive

b. pertaining to or characterized by the flesh or the body, its passions and appetites

c. an area of soft, muddy ground; swamp or swamplike region

d. to grant or give, as by favor, graciousness

e. the act or process of bettering; improvement

VOCABULARY 2. Use each word in a sentence of your own construction.

1. Vouchsafe –
   Your Sentence:

2. Slough –
   Your Sentence:

3. Betterment –
   Your Sentence:

4. Carnal –
   Your Sentence:

5. Indignation –
   Your Sentence:

The Pilgrim's Progress

| Book 1 Chapter 2 Worksheet 2 | Name |

Study Questions

1. Who is the Interpreter?

2. Who is the man pictured in the hallway in the house?

3. What purpose of the Law is contained in the illustration of the maid sweeping the house?

4. How does Patience portray a man of godly character? And how does Passion portray a man who is "of the world"?

5. What encouragement do you take from the man who fights through a company of soldiers to make it into the castle?

6. Describe the man in the iron cage. What biblical precedent do we have for the man in the iron cage? Does Bunyan believe you can lose your salvation? Take into account the illustration of the oil and the water in your answer.

The Pilgrim's Progress — Book 1, Chapter 3, Worksheet 1 — Name

VOCABULARY 1. Match the word with the correct definition

1. Sepulcher   a. intellectually or morally ignorant; unenlightened
2. Peradventure   b. a leafy, shady recess formed by tree branches, shrubs
3. Arbor   c. a tomb, grave, or burial place
4. Timorous   d. chance, doubt, or uncertainty
5. Benighted   e. full of fear; fearful

VOCABULARY 2. Use each word in a sentence of your own construction.

1. Sepulcher –
   Your Sentence:

2. Peradventure –
   Your Sentence:

3. Arbor –
   Your Sentence:

4. Timorous –
   Your Sentence:

Great Christian Classics: Four Essential Works of the Faith

5. Benighted –
   Your Sentence:

The Pilgrim's Progress | Book 1 Chapter 3 Worksheet 2 | Name

STUDY QUESTIONS

1. What significant things happened at the Cross for Christian? Is this the only visit to the Cross Christian makes on his journey to the Celestial City?

2. What does the roll represent?

3. Who are Simple, Sloth, and Presumption?

4. Who are Formalist and Hypocrisy? How do they manifest their true colors at the Hill Difficulty?

5. As you begin to meet these many false professors of the Christian faith on this journey, do you think Bunyan is exaggerating the problem of imposters and charlatan believers in the Church? Is the "Way" to heaven that narrow?

6. If the Christian is saved by faith alone, why does the journey to the Celestial City include trials such as the Hill Difficulty?

7. Why did Timorous and Mistrust turn back? What character qualities do they manifest?

8. What do we learn about rest on the Hill Difficulty? What is the Roll, and what does it mean when Christian left it at the arbor?

9. What is the House Beautiful?

10. Why were the lions placed before the house?

11. Who does Watchful the Porter represent, and how does he help the pilgrim?

12. Who are Discretion, Prudence, Piety, and Charity? Do they represent real people? What part do they play in the Church?

13. How does Christian testify concerning the change in his perceptions towards the world and towards the values and graces of God's kingdom?

14. What sort of encouragements did the pilgrim receive for his journey?

The Pilgrim's Progress — Book 1, Chapter 4, Worksheet 1 — Name

VOCABULARY 1. Match the word with the correct definition

1. Vainglory   a. quick and light in movement; moving with ease; agile

2. Nimbly   b. in a middle or unresolved position

3. Unutterable   c. something causing superstitious fear; a bogy

4. Hobgoblins   d. empty pomp or show

5. Betwixt   e. not communicable by utterance; unspeakable

VOCABULARY 2. Use each word in a sentence of your own construction.

1. Vainglory –
   Your Sentence:

2. Nimbly –
   Your Sentence:

3. Unutterable –
   Your Sentence:

4. Hobgoblins –
   Your Sentence:

5. Betwixt

   Your Sentence:

The Pilgrim's Progress — Book 1, Chapter 4, Worksheet 2 — Name

STUDY QUESTIONS

1. Who is Apollyon?

2. How does Apollyon attempt to discourage the pilgrim?

3. How does this battle with Apollyon portray the most significant spiritual battles fought in our own lives? Have you ever fought an Apollyon? How do you win these fights?

4. How does the Valley of the Shadow of Death compare to the Valley of Humiliation?

5. Why does Christian plunge on into the Valley of Humiliation despite the warning from the men escaping it?

6. What sort of trials await him in this valley?

7. What encouragement did he obtain for himself while in the thick of the valley?

8. How is it that Pagan and Pope are a little stiff in the joints? Is this an accurate portrayal for the Christian life today in places like China or Sweden or America?

The Pilgrim's Progress

**Book 1
Chapter 5
Worksheet 1**

Name

VOCABULARY 1. Match the word with the correct definition

1. Brimstone   a. to look with a sideways or oblique glance

2. Leered   b. to treat with insolence; bully; torment

3. Hectoring   c. a pretentious, swaggering display of courage

4. Bravadoes   d. sulfur

5. Prating   e. empty or foolish talk

VOCABULARY 2. Use each word in a sentence of your own construction.

1. Brimstone –
   Your Sentence:

2. Leered –
   Your Sentence:

3. Hectoring –
   Your Sentence:

4. Bravadoes –
   Your Sentence:

5. Prating –
   Your Sentence:

The Pilgrim's Progress

Book 1
Chapter 5
Worksheet 2

Name

STUDY QUESTIONS

1. What happens when Christian compares himself with his fellow believer, Faithful?

2. How is it that Faithful is not certain whether or not he entirely escaped the wiles of Wanton? Who is this Wanton, and how does she trip up young men who start on the pilgrim journey?

3. Is the influence of Adam and Moses upon Faithful positive or negative? Explain.

4. What sort of person in our day might the character Shame represent?

5. What is the problem with Talkative? What is his perspective of the relationship between faith and works?

The Pilgrim's Progress | Book 1 Chapter 6 Worksheet 1 | Name

VOCABULARY 1. Match the word with the correct definition

1. Vanity
2. Preferment
3. Raiment
4. Ignominy
5. Arraigned

a. a position or office affording social or pecuniary advancement

b. disgrace; dishonor; public contempt

c. to call or bring before a court to answer to an indictment

d. clothing; apparel; attire

e. excessive pride in one's appearance, qualities, abilities, achievements

VOCABULARY 2. Use each word in a sentence of your own construction.

1. Vanity –
   Your Sentence:

2. Preferment –
   Your Sentence:

3. Raiment –
   Your Sentence:

4. Ignominy –
   Your Sentence:

Great Christian Classics: Four Essential Works of the Faith 269

5. Arraigned –
   Your Sentence:

The Pilgrim's Progress

Book 1
Chapter 6
Worksheet 2

Name

Study Questions

1. What sort of exhortations does Evangelist give the pilgrims? Are these the sorts of exhortations we should receive in church services? Why or why not?

2. What is Vanity Fair, and how does the Bible view our relationship with the world? You will need to define "world."

3. Explain what Bunyan means when he speaks of the wares of Rome sold at the fair, merchandise that has been rejected by "our English nation."

4. Why does he speak of the national rows where various sorts of vanities are sold?

5. What are these vanities and why should Christians avoid buying them?

6. What three things set the pilgrims apart from the people at the Fair?

7. Why are they persecuted? Why are they hated so much?

8. Does Bunyan use satire in the depiction of the trial? If so, how does he use it? Does he use it effectively?

9. Summarize Faithful's defense at his trial.

10. Why did Christian escape martyrdom? How does Bunyan view the sovereignty of God over these persecutions?

The Pilgrim's Progress

Book 1
Chapter 7
Worksheet 1

Name

VOCABULARY 1. Match the word with the correct definition

1. Congee
2. Cozenage
3. Benefice
4. Lucre
5. Surfeits

a. a position or post granted to an ecclesiastic that guarantees a fixed amount of property or income

b. to take one's leave

c. to cheat, deceive, or trick

d. monetary reward or gain; money

e. excess; an excessive amount

VOCABULARY 2. Use each word in a sentence of your own construction.

1. Congee –
   Your Sentence:

2. Cozenage –
   Your Sentence:

3. Benefice –
   Your Sentence:

4. Lucre –
   Your Sentence:

Great Christian Classics: Four Essential Works of the Faith

5. Surfeits –
   Your Sentence:

The Pilgrim's Progress | Book 1 Chapter 7 Worksheet 2 | Name

STUDY QUESTIONS

1. Who are Mr. By-Ends, Mr. Save-all, and Mr. Love-Money? What is their fundamental problem? Do these men remind you of any present-day ministries?

2. What is a benefice, and what problem is Bunyan addressing in Mr. Money-Love's address?

3. How does this man's view of the ministry conflict with Paul's view in 1 Timothy 3:3? Do you think the man is greedy for filthy lucre? How can you tell?

4. Critique Christian's answer to the question relating to the seeking of the better benefice. Is he second-guessing motivations here or going to the heart of these men's issues?

5. Who is Demas, and what is his role in the story?

6. What lesson can the pilgrims learn from Lot's wife?

7. What led to the pilgrims veering out of the way at By-Path Meadow?

8. What do Doubting Castle and Giant Despair represent? In your opinion, is this a normal part of the Christian life?

9. What prevents the pilgrims from utter despair and even killing themselves?

10. How did the pilgrims escape the hands of the Giant?

The Pilgrim's Progress

Book 1
Chapter 8
Worksheet 1

Name

VOCABULARY 1. Match the word with the correct definition

1. Clamber
2. Dissemble
3. Gushing
4. Stile
5. Impediment

a. to put on the appearance of; feign
b. a series of steps or rungs by means of which a person may pass over a wall or fence
c. to climb, using both feet and hands; climb with effort or difficulty
d. obstruction; hindrance; obstacle
e. to flow out or issue suddenly, copiously, or forcibly

VOCABULARY 2. Use each word in a sentence of your own construction.

1. Clamber –
   Your Sentence:

2. Dissemble –
   Your Sentence:

3. Gushing –
   Your Sentence:

4. Stile –
   Your Sentence:

Great Christian Classics: Four Essential Works of the Faith   277

5. Impediment –
   Your Sentence:

The Pilgrim's Progress | Book 1 Chapter 8 Worksheet 2 | Name

Study Questions

1. Who are the Shepherds, and what are they doing on the Delectable Mountains?

2. How do the Shepherds issue warnings to the Pilgrims?

The Pilgrim's Progress

Book 1
Chapter 9
Worksheet 1

Name

VOCABULARY 1. Match the word with the correct definition

1. Scramble
2. Doleful
3. Pawn
4. Amendments
5. Divers

a. several; various; sundry
b. to pledge; stake; risk
c. to climb or move quickly using one's hands and feet
d. a change made by correction, addition, or deletion
e. sorrowful; mournful; melancholy

VOCABULARY 2. Use each word in a sentence of your own construction.

1. Scramble –
   Your Sentence:

2. Doleful –
   Your Sentence:

3. Pawn –
   Your Sentence:

4. Amendments –
   Your Sentence:

5. Divers –

Your Sentence:

The Pilgrim's Progress

Book 1
Chapter 9
Worksheet 2

Name

STUDY QUESTIONS

1. What contrast might we draw between Little-Faith and Turn-Away?

2. What part does Great-Grace play in the life of men like Little-Faith?

3. Why is the false teacher in black given the name "Flatterer"?

4. Why do the pilgrims spend so little time talking to the Atheist?

5. What are the sins that Hopeful associates with Vanity Fair and general worldliness?

6. Why is it inappropriate to sleep when traversing the Enchanted Ground? How does this pertain to your Christian walk?

7. What do Christian and Hopeful do to stay awake in the Enchanted Ground?

8. How did Hopeful embark on the pilgrim journey?

9. What are Ignorance's character issues?

10. What are Ignorance's doctrinal problems?

The Pilgrim's Progress

Book 1
Chapter 10
Worksheet 1

Name

VOCABULARY 1. Match the word with the correct definition

1. Contemptible
2. Pangs
3. Dainties
4. Tarry
5. Despond

a. pleasing to the taste and, often, temptingly served or delicate

b. to be depressed by loss of hope, confidence, or courage

c. a sudden, brief, sharp pain or physical sensation

d. deserving of or held in contempt; despicable

e. to remain or stay, as in a place; sojourn

VOCABULARY 2. Use each word in a sentence of your own construction.

1. Contemptible –
   Your Sentence:

2. Pangs –
   Your Sentence:

3. Dainties –
   Your Sentence:

4. Tarry –
   Your Sentence:

5. Despond –
   Your Sentence:

The Pilgrim's Progress

Book 1
Chapter 10
Worksheet 2

Name

STUDY QUESTIONS

1. According to Christian's explanation, why is Ignorance so ignorant?

2. What is the process of apostasy as described by the pilgrims? Is this biblically accurate?

3. What does the river signify?

4. How does Bunyan describe the Celestial City, and is it a biblically accurate view?

5. What insights can you derive from John Bunyan in his closing poem?

The Pilgrim's Progress | Book 2 / The Author's Way / Worksheet 1 | Name

Study Questions

1. Who or what is Bunyan interacting with in the opening poem?

2. What do you think is the purpose of this poem?

3. How were John Bunyan's pilgrims received in the countries mentioned in the poem?

The Pilgrim's Progress — Book 2, To The Reader, Worksheet 1 — Name

VOCABULARY 1. Match the word with the correct definition

1. Fancy   a. any great number of persons or things; multitude

2. Legions   b. imagination or fantasy

3. Bosom   c. depressed; sad

4. Carriage   d. the breast of a human being

5. Dumpish   e. comportment, demeanor

VOCABULARY 2. Use each word in a sentence of your own construction.

1. Fancy –
   Your Sentence:

2. Legions –
   Your Sentence:

3. Bosom –
   Your Sentence:

4. Carriage –
   Your Sentence:

5. Dumpish –
   Your Sentence:

The Pilgrim's Progress — Book 2, To The Reader, Worksheet 2 — Name

STUDY QUESTIONS

1. What was it that convicted Christiana to embark on the journey with her children?

2. How were the initial exhortations and encouragements for Christiana different from what her husband had received from Evangelist?

The Pilgrim's Progress | Book 2 Chapter 1 Worksheet 1 | Name

VOCABULARY 1. Match the word with the correct definition

1. Slough
2. Sagacity
3. Obeisance
4. Lumbering
5. Amiss

a. acuteness of mental discernment and soundness of judgment
b. a movement of the body expressing deep respect or deferential courtesy
c. improperly; wrongly
d. an area of soft, muddy ground; swamp or swamplike region
e. to heap together in disorder

VOCABULARY 2. Use each word in a sentence of your own construction.

1. Slough –
   Your Sentence:

2. Sagacity –
   Your Sentence:

3. Obeisance –
   Your Sentence:

4. Lumbering –
   Your Sentence:

5. Amiss –

   Your Sentence:

The Pilgrim's Progress

Book 2
Chapter 1
Worksheet 2

Name

STUDY QUESTIONS

1. Why did Mercy choose to go with Christiana?

2. What is the main accusation that the neighbor women bring against Christiana for choosing to go after her husband on this pilgrim pathway? Do Christians still receive these forms of accusations today?

3. Who are those who have worked to fill in the Slough of Despond on the King's Highway, and what do they fill it in with? Explain the metaphor.

4. What is the significance of knocking at the gate? Do we find here initial indications of faith? Is it possible that some might become discouraged when they are not received immediately into the way? What test of faith is set forth at the gate?

The Pilgrim's Progress

Book 2 Chapter 2 Worksheet 1

Name

VOCABULARY 1. Match the word with the correct definition

1. Chide
2. Scuffle
3. Proffered
4. Disparagement
5. Churl

a. a rude, boorish, or surly person
b. an offer or proposal
c. to express disapproval of; scold; reproach
d. to speak of or treat slightly; depreciate; belittle
e. to struggle or fight in a rough, confused manner

VOCABULARY 2. Use each word in a sentence of your own construction.

1. Chide –
   Your Sentence:

2. Scuffle –
   Your Sentence:

3. Proffered –
   Your Sentence:

4. Disparagement –
   Your Sentence:

5. Churl –

    Your Sentence:

The Pilgrim's Progress — Book 2, Chapter 2, Worksheet 2 — Name

STUDY QUESTIONS

1. What lesson is Bunyan driving home with the boys' eating the fruit hanging over the fence?

2. What is the intent of the two "ill-favored ones?" Do you think women have always faced this kind of oppression? What does this say about the Christian life in general? What is the purpose of including this incident at this point in the story?

3. What was the reception like at the House of the Interpreter? Why was there such a reception?

4. What can we learn from Matthew 21:29 in relation to sharing the Gospel with others?

5. How does the man with the muck-rake provide a great picture of most of the people who live about us in our neighborhoods?

6. Do you think the illustration given for Proverbs 30:28 is an accurate or inaccurate interpretation of the text? Why or why not?

7. Find at least two references in Scripture that compare us to sheep. In what ways are we compared to sheep? How should Christians be like sheep when they suffer and die?

8. What is the fruit that God wants us to bear in our lives?

9. In what situation might the robin gobble down a spider? How is this a good test for genuine faith in our own lives?

10. What do the illustrations of the tree, the robin, and the dunged field have in common? What is the Interpreter attempting to do with these illustrations?

11. What does the dinner meal entertainment reveal of the culture during Bunyan's day?

12. What is illustrated by the bath and the Passover seal which the family received before leaving the House of the Interpreter?

The Pilgrim's Progress | Book 2 Chapter 3 Worksheet 1 | Name

VOCABULARY 1. Match the word with the correct definition

1. Efficacious   a. joyous, merry, or gay in disposition

2. Blithe   b. capable of having the desired result or effect

3. Meddlesome   c. a journey, especially a long one, made to some sacred place

4. Pilgrimage   d. a leafy, shady recess formed by tree branches, shrubs

5. Arbor   e. given to meddling; interfering; intrusive

VOCABULARY 2. Use each word in a sentence of your own construction.

1. Efficacious –
   Your Sentence:

2. Blithe –
   Your Sentence:

3. Meddlesome –
   Your Sentence:

4. Pilgrimage –
   Your Sentence:

5. Arbor –
   Your Sentence:

The Pilgrim's Progress — Book 2, Chapter 3, Worksheet 2

STUDY QUESTIONS

1. Who is Great-Heart and, what part does he play in Christiana's journey?

2. How does Christiana's experience at the Cross differ from her husband's?

3. Extra Challenge: Does the bath and the seal received at the House of the Interpreter contribute in any way to the difference mentioned in question 2?

4. According to Great-Heart, how is our sin forgiven?

5. Why is the place of rest on the Hill Difficulty always the place of forgetfulness? What is the point expressed here?

The Pilgrim's Progress | Book 2 Chapter 4 Worksheet 1 | Name

VOCABULARY 1. Match the word with the correct definition

1. Cringe   a. bold, brave, or dauntless

2. Stoutly   b. any medicine; a drug or medicament

3. Damsel   c. a preceding circumstance, event, object, style, phenomenon

4. Antecedent   d. to shrink, bend, or crouch, especially in fear or servility; cower

5. Physic   e. a young woman or girl; a maiden

VOCABULARY 2. Use each word in a sentence of your own construction.

1. Cringe –
   Your Sentence:

2. Stoutly –
   Your Sentence:

3. Damsel –
   Your Sentence:

4. Antecedent –
   Your Sentence:

5. Physic –
   Your Sentence:

The Pilgrim's Progress — Book 2, Chapter 4, Worksheet 2 — Name

STUDY QUESTIONS

1. Cultural Setting: What was the bottle of spirits?

2. If the lions characterize trying circumstances, who is this Giant Grim? How do Christians deal with their fear?

3. Cultural Setting: What did families do around the dinner table and after dinner?

4. Does the house Beautiful characterize Christian Hospitality in a home or a church meeting? Why?

5. What is Prudence doing with the boys? What form of education is this, and where do we find it in the Bible or in Christian history?

6. What is Mercy's gift that she exercises in the House Beautiful?

7. What is Mr. Brisk's focus in life, and why does Mercy refuse him?

8. What is the fruit of Beelzebub? How do children in Christian homes today consume this fruit?

9. How was Matthew cured of the gripes? What is ex carne et Sanguine Christi? How do we cure our children after they have consumed the fruit of Beelzebub?

The Pilgrim's Progress

Book 2 Chapter 5 Worksheet 1

Name

VOCABULARY 1. Match the word with the correct definition

1. Fray   a. a diabolically cruel or wicked person

2. Intimation   b. disgusting; revolting; repulsive

3. Fiend   c. a fight, battle, or skirmish

4. Loathsome   d. to take part in a matter, especially officiously

5. Intermeddle   e. making known indirectly

VOCABULARY 2. Use each word in a sentence of your own construction.

1. Fray –
   Your Sentence:

2. Intimation –
   Your Sentence:

3. Fiend –
   Your Sentence:

4. Loathsome –
   Your Sentence:

5. Intermeddle –
   Your Sentence:

The Pilgrim's Progress — Book 2, Chapter 5, Worksheet 2 — Name

Study Questions

1. Why did Christian meet Apollyon in this Valley of Humiliation? What is the best way to make it through the Valley of Humiliation?

2. What does it take to make it through the Valley of the Shadow of Death?

3. Who is the Giant Maul? How do people today get taken down by this giant?

The Pilgrim's Progress — Book 2, Chapter 6, Worksheet 1 — Name

VOCABULARY 1. Match the word with the correct definition

1. Detriment   a. a leader, guide, director, or manager

2. Girdle   b. depression or lowness of spirits

3. Conductor   c. a rectangular or circular flat piece of wood on which food is served or carved

4. Dejection   d. loss, damage, disadvantage, or injury

5. Trencher   e. a belt, cord, sash, or the like, worn about the waist

VOCABULARY 2. Use each word in a sentence of your own construction.

1. Detriment –
   Your Sentence:

2. Girdle –
   Your Sentence:

3. Conductor –
   Your Sentence:

4. Dejection –
   Your Sentence:

5. Trencher –
   Your Sentence:

The Pilgrim's Progress — Book 2, Chapter 7, Worksheet 1 — Name

VOCABULARY 1. Match the word with the correct definition

1. Conferred
2. Cote
3. Palate
4. Diffidence
5. Jocund

a. the roof of the mouth

b. lacking confidence in one's own ability or worth

c. a shelter, coop, or small shed for sheep, pigs, pigeons

d. to consult together; compare opinions; carry on a discussion or deliberation

e. cheerful; merry; gay; blithe

VOCABULARY 2. Use each word in a sentence of your own construction.

1. Conferred –
   Your Sentence:

2. Cote –
   Your Sentence:

3. Palate –
   Your Sentence:

4. Diffidence –
   Your Sentence:

Great Christian Classics: Four Essential Works of the Faith   311

5. Jocund –
    Your Sentence:

The Pilgrim's Progress

Book 2
Chapter 7
Worksheet 2

Name

STUDY QUESTIONS

1. Honest hails from a town farther from the sun than the City of Destruction. What wisdom about the world does this provide us?

2. Describe Mr. Fearing. How is it that men like Mr. Fearing survive the journey? Why does he survive it and others, who seem more promising, do not make it?

3. Cultural Setting: What is the bass and the sack-but? Comment on Bunyan's ideas of music. What sort of music did Mr. Fearing prefer?

4. What is the proper role that fear plays in the Christian life?

5. What would Self-Will say about David's sin with Bathsheba or Solomon's many wives? What is Self-Will's basic problem?

6. Cultural Setting: How were men and women matched for marriage in the story?

7. What sort of things did Gaius like to do in his home? What does this teach us concerning Christian home life?

8. What characterizes Mr. Ready-to-Halt and Mr. Feeble-Mind? How do they differ from each other?

The Pilgrim's Progress

Book 2
Chapter 8
Worksheet 1

Name

VOCABULARY 1. Match the word with the correct definition

1. Incommodity
2. Pragmatic
3. Bliss
4. Smother
5. Dismal

a. pertaining to a practical point of view or practical considerations
b. supreme happiness; utter joy or contentment
c. gloomy; dreary; cheerless
d. disadvantage; inconvenience
e. to stifle or suffocate

VOCABULARY 2. Use each word in a sentence of your own construction.

1. Incommodity –
   Your Sentence:

2. Pragmatic –
   Your Sentence:

3. Bliss –
   Your Sentence:

4. Smother –
   Your Sentence:

Great Christian Classics: Four Essential Works of the Faith

5. Dismal –
   Your Sentence:

The Pilgrim's Progress — Book 2, Chapter 8, Worksheet 2

STUDY QUESTIONS

1. Who is Mnason in the Bible, and how does he fit into this story?

2. Why did Vanity Fair stop persecuting Christians? Do cities in your state or country persecute Christians? Why or why not?

3. Does it seem strange to you to find some good men living in Vanity Fair? Is it possible for this to happen? Why or why not?

4. What is this dragon that lures children out of the village to prey upon them? Reference biblical allusions to the Dragon.

5. What biblical basis do we have for committing babies or little children to the arms of Jesus?

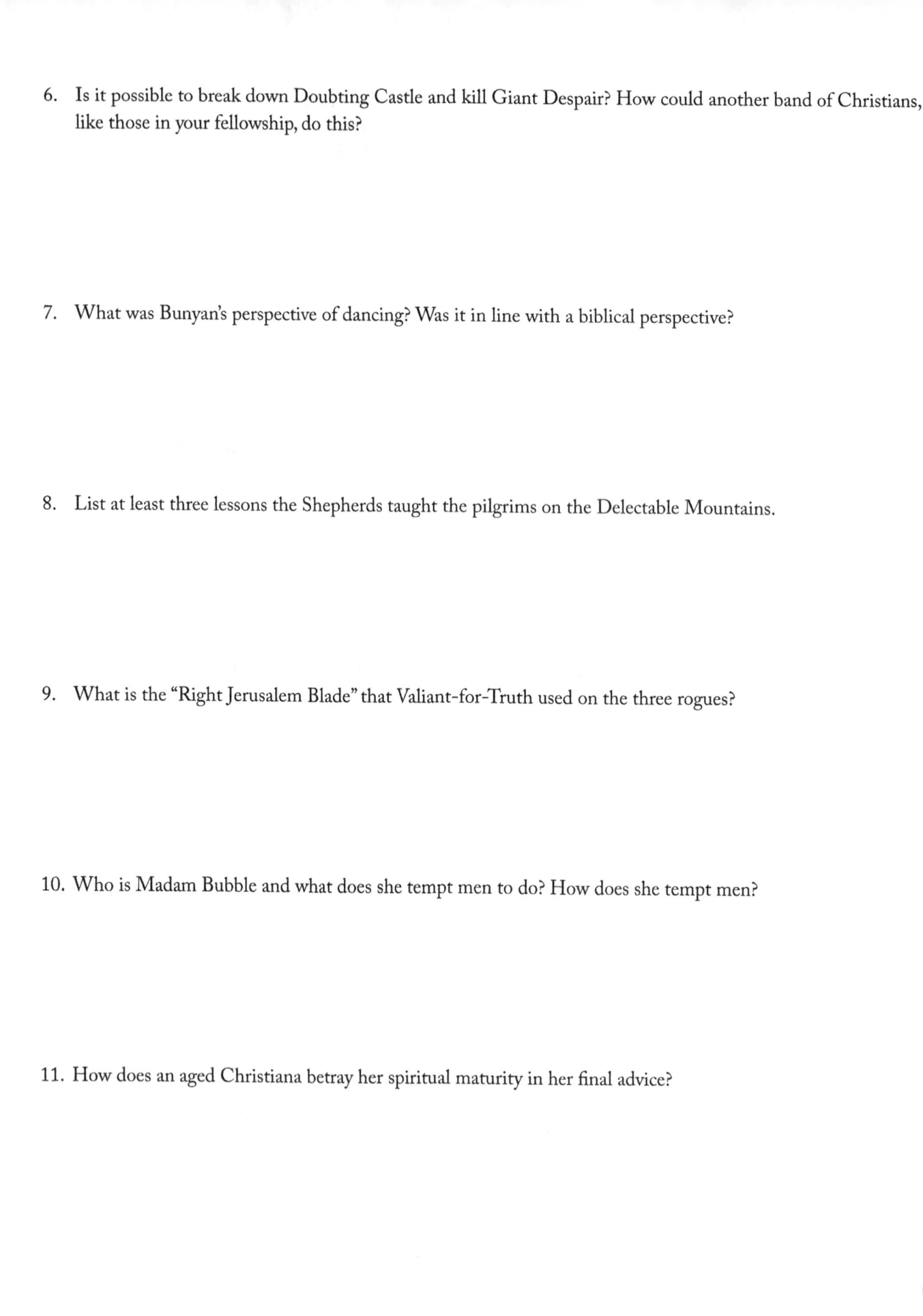

6. Is it possible to break down Doubting Castle and kill Giant Despair? How could another band of Christians, like those in your fellowship, do this?

7. What was Bunyan's perspective of dancing? Was it in line with a biblical perspective?

8. List at least three lessons the Shepherds taught the pilgrims on the Delectable Mountains.

9. What is the "Right Jerusalem Blade" that Valiant-for-Truth used on the three rogues?

10. Who is Madam Bubble and what does she tempt men to do? How does she tempt men?

11. How does an aged Christiana betray her spiritual maturity in her final advice?

12. How does the final welcome at the Celestial City manifest the great joy, glory, and love that awaits the weary warrior?

The Pilgrim's Progress | Essay | Name

ESSAY ASSIGNMENT Provide a 500-word essay on **one** of the following subject areas.

1. Does John Bunyan think you can "lose your salvation"?
2. What is salvation according to this allegory?
3. Is this an accurate portrayal of the Christian life? Is the Christian life as dangerous, and is the way as narrow as he presents it? Does such a story encourage people in their faith, or does it tempt them to doubt their salvation?
4. What is the significance of leaving the City of Destruction behind? At several points, the pilgrims claim to no longer belong to the devil—what is the significance of this allegiance in this tale?
5. Give several examples of where the more pleasant parts of the journey are quickly followed by a severe trial of some sort. Is this a pattern?
6. Does the Church play a part in this tale or is it all about the individual's relationship to God?
7. Does Christian impact the world as a puritan or does he escape the world as a separatist? Does *Pilgrim's Progress* give us a balanced perspective on how to live in the world, but not be of the world? And what is that balanced perspective?
8. How would you characterize Christian's relationship with Faithful? How about his relationship with Hopeful?
9. How does John Bunyan perceive natural man? Does he believe that man is totally depraved and unable to even take the first step to save himself without the working of God's grace? How does John Bunyan speak of the sovereignty of God in these tales?
10. What is John Bunyan's perception of the Old Testament Law of God? How does he present the relationship between law and grace?
11. How does Mr. Great-Heart play the part of a pastor through the journey in the second book?
12. What are the major differences between the first book and the second book of *Pilgrim's Progress*?

| The Pilgrim's Progress | Exam | Scope: Bunyan | Total score: ____ of 100 | Name |

MULTIPLE CHOICE Circle all that apply. (5 points each)

1. What literary form is The Pilgrim's Progress written in?
    A. Poetry
    B. Prose
    C. Allegory
    D. Play

2. Where does Christian meet Hopeful?
    A. City of Destruction
    B. Town of Morality
    C. House of the Interpreter
    D. Vanity Fair

3. What does the "roll" represent?
    A. Assurance of eternal life and acceptance into heaven
    B. Justification by faith alone
    C. The cross of Christ
    D. The Word of God

4. What is the name of Christian's companion before leaving Vanity Fair?
    A. Hopeful
    B. Pliable
    C. Faithful
    D. Evangelist

5. What final place did Christian have to cross over to reach the Celestial City?
    A. The Delectable Mountains
    B. The River
    C. The Enchanted Ground
    D. The Slough of Despond

6. Who is rejected entrance at the Celestial Gate?
    A. Ignorance
    B. Talkative
    C. Mr. Worldly Wiseman
    D. Mr. By-Ends

Great Christian Classics: Four Essential Works of the Faith

7. What is the name of Christian's wife?
   A. Hopeful
   B. Christiana
   C. Patience
   D. Piety

8. Who does Christian meet at the wicket-gate?
   A. Faithful
   B. Mr. Worldly Wiseman
   C. Obstinate
   D. Good-will

9. In what location do Christian and Hopeful almost lose their lives?
   A. Vanity Fair
   B. Doubting Castle
   C. Slough of Despond
   D. Valley of the Shadow of Death

10. What are the names of three witnesses at the trial in Vanity Fair?
    A. Envy, Ignorance, and Malice
    B. Envy, Malice, and Superstition
    C. Envy, Ignorance, and Pickthank
    D. Envy, Superstition, and Pickthank

11. Who catechises the sons of Christiana?
    A. Great-Heart
    B. Prudence
    C. Mercy
    D. Mr. Honest

12. How many sons did Christiana have?
    A. 2
    B. 3
    C. 4
    D. 6

Fill in the Blank

1. Christian enters the path through the_____ gate.
2. Christian flees to the Celestial City from the City of_____.
3. The name of Christian's two companions during his journey are_____and_____.
4. In the second part, the protector of the pilgrims is named_____.

Short Answer

1. From where did Bunyan write *The Pilgrim's Progress*?

2. In the first part, who does Christian leave behind in the City of Destruction?

3. In the second part, what happens to Giant Despair and Doubting Castle?

Worksheet Answer Key

ON THE INCARNATION

CHAPTER 1 - CREATION AND THE FALL

Vocabulary
1. Traduce - to expose to shame or blame by means of falsehood and misrepresentation
2. Wiseacres - a person who possesses or affects to possess great wisdom.
3. Impute - to attribute or ascribe
4. Artificer - a skillful or artistic worker; craftsperson

Questions
1. He discussed the subjects of idolatry and the divinity of Christ.
2. Macarius. The man is a true lover of Christ.
3. They deride the doctrine.
4. The weakness of the cross destroys the pomp and parade of idols. Christ actually wins over those that mock him, in a surreptitious way.
5. He did it out of the love and goodness of God towards sinful men, in order to bring about their salvation.
6. He is the agent of creation and salvation.
7. They teach that there is no personal mind behind the universe. The universe created itself, and everything is haphazard.
8. The haphazard nature of creation would never have produced parts that function within a whole (like the human body does).
9. God created things out of preexistent matter.
10. To deny God as the Creator of matter, is to deny that God is ultimately God. It is to limit God, and to limit God is to deny His very "godness."
11. They distinguish a Creator apart from the Father of our Lord Jesus Christ. They point to some other god, as having created the world.
12. He uses a Bible verse, pointing out that the NT God is no different from the OT Creator God (Matt. 19:4-6, also John 1:3).
13. Man was created in the image of God. They are able to express the mind of God (though in a limited degree).
14. He would continue in a state of death and corruption, under the complete dominion of death. Death is "returning to non-existence."
15. An embodied spirit.
16. Evil is non-being, the negation of what is good.
17. Adultery, theft, and murder. But worst of all, homosexuality. He calls these crimes contrary to nature.
18. Matthew, John, Genesis, Hebrews, Psalms, and Romans, Shepherd of Hermas and Wisdom

CHAPTER 2 - THE DIVINE DILEMMA AND ITS SOLUTION IN THE INCARNATION (PART I)

Vocabulary
1. Incorporeal - not corporeal or material; insubstantial
2. Incorruptible - will not dissolve, disintegrate, decay
3. Liability - debts or pecuniary obligations
4. Untainted - no trace of infection, contamination, or the like
5. Appropriation - setting apart, authorizing, or legislating for some specific purpose or use
6. Incurred - to become liable or subject to through one's own action

Questions
1. Because He could not go back on His word.
2. Because man had "shared the nature of the Word." God had created him in His own image. God's goodness would have required a salvation scheme for man.
3. Man could not save himself by repenting, because repentance cannot change the corruption of his nature. Moreover, the corruption of man's nature powerfully controlled him, and there was for him no saving grace.
4. He would have to recreate us (as He created us once before). He would have to suffer for us. He would reconcile us to God the Father.
5. Somebody had to die in order to release us from corruption, and He would have to rise from the dead to overcome death. Jesus had to take on a human body, because His God nature could not possibly undergo death.
6. Athanasius illustrates it by the king who moves into a city, and his very presence in the city reduces the incidence of crime. Jesus similarly, broke the back of death and corruption, enabling us to live with Him.
7. Jesus put an end to the law of death that bound us. And, He gave us new life and the hope of the resurrection.

CHAPTER 3 - THE DIVINE DILEMMA AND ITS SOLUTION IN THE INCARNATION (PART II)

Vocabulary
1. Impiety - lack of piety; lack of reverence for God or sacred things; irreverence
2. Immolated - to destroy by fire
3. Colonize - to form a colony
4. Obliterate - to remove or destroy all traces of; do away with; destroy completely
5. Paradox - a statement or proposition that seems self-contradictory or absurd but in reality expresses a possible truth
6. Faculty (Ability) - an ability, natural or acquired, for a particular kind of action

Questions
1. Man can know his Creator
2. He says that Christ is the "Image Absolute."
3. Men preferred idolatry over the truth. They engaged in human sacrifice to their false gods. They practiced the magic arts, subjected themselves to the deceit of demons, and involved themselves in astrology. They could not believe anything existed outside of that which they could see. They turned into materialists.
4. The fact that they themselves were created in the image of God. - The works of Creation gave them knowledge of God. - Certain prophets (Noah, Moses, etc.)

communicated the truth to them. - God gave the law to both Jews and Gentiles through Noah, Moses, and others.
5. They were blinded by the pleasures of the moments, demonic deceptions by their own wickedness.
6. They were not made in God's image.
7. He speaks of a picture painted on a wall, that has been marred, scraped, and vandalized over time. Eventually, you can hardly tell what was painted there, until the painter paints the picture over again.
8. Men were blinded, and they were no match for the deception of evil spirits.
9. Because men have wallowed in wickedness. Men were looking the opposite direction.
10. He is a simple teacher, and teaches by life lessons (in his life and words).
11. He cast out demons, and thereby proved them to be poor excuses for gods. He dispensed of hero worship and man worship by rising from the dead (something that man could never do).
12. That Christ the Person (the Word), was not limited by his body. When He moved around in His body, He did not cease from directing the whole universe. The universe could not contain Him; in fact He contained the universe! He was within the universe and outside the universe at the same time.
13. He orders, directs, and gives life to all. He is sovereign over every single detail of the universe. This is very essential to the Godhood of Christ.
14. He was born of a woman. He ate food.
15. He healed the man born blind. He turned water into wine. He created food to feed 5,000 people. He walked on water. He had to be the Creator of the earth and Master of all the physical elements.

CHAPTER 4 - THE DEATH OF CHRIST

Vocabulary
1. Primal - first; original; primeval
2. Banished - to compel to depart; send, drive, or put away
3. Dissolution - the act or process of resolving or dissolving into parts or elements
4. Consonant - in agreement; agreeable; in accord; consistent
5. Annulled - to make void or null; abolish; cancel
6. Antagonists - a person who is opposed to, struggles against, or competes with another; opponent; adversary

Questions
1. The earth quaked. The mountains were torn asunder.
2. He believed the Word of God as he read it in the Gospel accounts.
3. Jesus' death on the cross.
4. Athanasius says that Jesus died for "all."
5. It was mortal, having been conceived of a woman. But, the indwelling of the Word provided for its "incorruptibility."
6. An ordinary death would have made him out to be an ordinary man. He had the ability to heal others, surely he could have healed himself. Yet, He had to die as a sacrifice for sin. He needed witnesses to His death, and an assurance of death - and the Roman authorities made sure of that. This precluded Him faking His death. His resurrection had to be a very public affair. If He had control over His own death, people would suspect the genuineness of His death.
7. That Christ suffered an ignominious death at the hands of enemies, in order that His resurrection might prove itself to be even more magnificent.
8. According to Gal. 3:13, Christ was made a curse for us, and a crucifixion is considered a curse in and of itself.
9. Christ's "lifting up" in the air took him to the real battle - the battle with the prince of the power of the air.

CHAPTER 5 - THE RESURRECTION

Vocabulary
1. Impassable - unable to be surmounted
2. Deriders – Those who laugh in scorn or contempt; scoff or jeer at; mock
3. Vanquished - to conquer or subdue by superior force, as in battle
4. Bereft - deprived; parted from
5. Ostentation - pretentious or conspicuous show, as of wealth or importance; display intended to impress others
6. Pursuance - the following or carrying out of some plan, course, injunction, or the like
7. Irrefragable - not to be disputed or contested

Questions
1. He wanted to be sure they knew the body was dead, but He didn't want to wait so long that they would forget about His death.
2. They despised death. They didn't think twice about being put to death because they were confident in their own resurrection.
3. They mock at it as a dead thing robbed of its strength.
4. They look beyond this present life, and train themselves to die.
5. We believe in the death and resurrection of Christ, and subject ourselves to persecution.
6. By the sign of the cross and the faith of Christ.
7. This is a tracing of a cross using the hand, thumb, or fingers across the forehead or across the body. It signified a belief in the power of the cross of Christ. Answers may vary on legitimacy. The Bible does not command the use of this symbol. Nonetheless, Christians have put symbols of fish and crosses on their homes, churches, etc.
8. He sees the serpent's head as crushed, and the lion as (at the very least) maimed. These represent the devil (in Scripture). (1 Pet. 5:8, Rev. 12:9, 20:2).
9. Christ's death destroyed death. His resurrection only displayed the victory (or celebrated it).
10. He turns real people from adultery, murder, and idolatry to serve the living and true God. Wherever Christ is named, idolatry is destroyed and the fraud of demons exposed. A dead man cannot prick the consciences of

men!
11. We do not call Christ dead. We call death dead. We call evil spirits and idols dead.
12. We learn about Him through His works.
13. They deny it because they are blind to it. We still see instances where the resurrection life of Christ works in men. But in an apostasy, the message gets a little cloudy.

CHAPTER 6 - REFUTATION OF THE JEWS

Vocabulary
1. Incongruity - out of keeping or place; inappropriate; unbecoming
2. Surmises - a conjecture or opinion
3. Despoiling - to strip of possessions, things of value, etc.; rob; plunder; pillage
4. Implacable - not to be appeased, mollified, or pacified
5. Brazenly - shameless or impudent
6. Demented - crazy; insane; mad

Questions
1. He points to Old Testament prophecy.
2. Isaiah 7:14, Numbers 24:17, Numbers 24:5-7, Isaiah 8:4, Isaiah 19:1, Hosea 11:1
3. Isaiah 53
4. He was born of a virgin. A star announced His birth.
5. He overcame idolatry in Egypt. It happened with the dawning of Christianity.
6. Deut. 28:66, Ps. 22:16-18, Is. 11:10
7. Jesus died on a cross. A star announced His birth. Persians came to His birth. The heathen Egyptians turned from their idolatry when Jesus Christ came to them. They were witnessing this in Athanasius' day.
8. Because Christ was the only miracle-worker that restored a man's sight (who was born blind). Christ also helped a lame man to walk.
9. The Christ is referred to as the Holy One of holies. That Christ would be the end of prophecy (which is what happened). The holy city would remain until Christ appeared.
10. Obviously, all of this stopped with Christ. He was the final King, Prophet, and Vision.
11. Much of the heathen idolatrous practices have gone away. These things happened because of Christ.
12. "He has enlightened all men everywhere... The whole earth is filled with the knowledge of God... The Gentiles are forsaking idolatry..." It is rare to find this level of optimism in our day, although we are seeing Christ's imprint on the whole world in a fuller sense today (than Athanasius saw in his day). The faith of the author, and the faith of all of us, can be seen in how we recognize the fingerprints of Jesus Christ on the whole world.

CHAPTER 7 - REFUTATION OF THE GENTILES (PART I)

Vocabulary
1. Confute - to prove (a person) to be wrong by argument or proof
2. Actuate - to incite or move to action; impel; motivate
3. Pervades - to become spread throughout all parts of
4. Vitiate - to impair the quality of; make faulty; spoil
5. Intrinsic - belonging to a thing by its very nature
6. Endued - to invest or endow with some gift, quality, or faculty
7. Thrall - a person who is in bondage; slave

Questions
1. He challenges the fool in his folly. He points out the foolishness of the idolatry of the Gentiles and then shows the reasonableness of his own perspective.
2. He points out that if Christ could enter the world (that is a created place of space and time), then he could enter the material body of a human.
3. If the Word can actuate all of creation, of course He could actuate a distinct human body in that creation.
4. He wanted to minister to men. He didn't come to "dazzle" them.
5. He argues that Plato allowed for God to take the driver's seat of the universe and steer it aright in order to save the universe. If Plato allows for this, then why can't the Word take on human flesh?
6. The circumstances are different in the two cases. Creation and healing are two different things. Also, death and sin had corrupted the inside of the body. Therefore, life had to enter the body in order to bring about life in the body (where there was only death).
7. He shows that He is master over the water, demons, and death (by His resurrection).

CHAPTER 8 - REFUTATION OF THE GENTILES (PART II)

Vocabulary
1. Spurn - to reject with disdain; scorn
2. Attest - to bear witness to; certify; declare to be correct, true, or genuine
3. Chastity - undefiled or stainless
4. Imposture - the action or practice of imposing fraudulently upon others
5. Sophists - a person who reasons adroitly and speciously rather than soundly
6. Compunction - any uneasiness or hesitation about the rightness of an action
7. Disrepute - bad repute; low regard; disfavor
8. Transcend - to rise above or go beyond; overpass; exceed
9. Epiphany - an appearance or manifestation, especially of a deity

Questions
1. The Greek and Roman gods are losing status fast. People are turning from idolatry all over the world. Pagan prophecies have ceased and idolatry is ceasing.
2. Delphi, Dordona, Boeotia, Lycia, Libya, Egypt, and those of the Kabiri and Pythoness.
3. People from Chaldea, Egypt, and India.

4. Noisy talk. The Greeks really never convinced very many people on their theories and ethics.
5. Christ has changed people's lives and instituted moral and well-grounded lives everywhere on the basis of very simple teaching.
6. Martyrs, and men and women who take on a life of celibacy
7. Demons are routed by the sign of the cross and the mention of Christ. These are symbols and words that stand for the power of the death and resurrection of Christ in the mind of believers. Communicating words and symbols (while believing strongly in what they stand for) really does bring about good effects. The assumption of course, is that they are believing what they are saying. If the sign of the cross is just a superstitious symbol that doesn't stand for a reality believed, then it is useless.
8. Christ destroys magic and magicians.
9. He drives demons out. How can a house divided against itself stand? (Luke 11:17-18).
10. Christ didn't need to use herbs that were already created for the purpose of helping the healing process. Christ created new flesh, bone, etc. ex nihilo in his healing.
11. Dionysus encouraged men to drunkenness. Christ actually does something far more difficult. He makes a drunkard sober for a lifetime.
12. The Greek philosophers could never agree with each other. They constantly declaimed each other.
13. The faith of Christ and the sign of the cross brought them to give up their madness and constantly murderous ways.
14. Nothing. They couldn't think of any possibility for a resurrection.
15. Hyrcania (Turkmenistan), Armenia, Ethiopia (Sudan), Scythia (Kazakhstan), etc.
16. The places were anarchical. It was dangerous. You had to defend yourself with swords and knives.
17. Isaiah 2:4 (sometimes referred to as a millennial Scripture) "And he shall judge among the nations, and shall rebuke many people: and they shall beat their swords into plowshares, and their spears into pruninghooks: nation shall not lift up sword against nation, neither shall they learn war any more."
18. We fight by integrity of soul, virtuous action, and self-discipline. As young men, they do not give way to sexual sin.
19. They prefer to study the Gospels over all of the wisdom of the Greeks.
20. Psalm 100:3 distinguishes between man and God. The Bible speaks of us having fellowship with God (1 John 1:6), but we do not become God. Later formulations were a little more careful - two natures, one person without confusion, change, separation.
21. It is disappearing. Aristotle was revived in the 1100s and 1200s, largely through the influence of men like Thomas Aquinas.
22. Mark 3:27 and Rev. 20:1-3.

CHAPTER 9 - CONCLUSION
Questions
1. There were martyrs who taught him the Scriptures.
2. It will be a coming in glory. It will be a coming that will bring the resurrection and incorruptibility to all. He will judge the world, and send some to heaven and others to hell.
3. We must come at it with a purified soul and a good life.
4. One who loves God and lives a godly life.

EXAM
Multiple Choice
1. C
2. D
3. A, C
4. C
5. A, D

True/False
6. T
7. F
8. T
9. T
10. F

Short Answer
11. Homosexuality
12. Christ is low key, unpretentious, and he actually changes people's lives. The Greek philosophers could not do this.
13. The Scriptures present him as born of a virgin, and he ate food like a man.
14. Turkmenistan, Kazakhstan, Armenia, Sudan

Match
15. c
16. d
17. a
18. e
19. f
20. b

THE IMITATION OF CHRIST

BOOK ONE VOCABULARY 1
1. b
2. g
3. f
4. c
5. e
6. a
7. d

BOOK ONE VOCABULARY 2
1. c
2. e
3. b

4. g
5. f
   d
   a

BOOK ONE QUESTIONS

Section 1
1. A'Kempis believes that the walk will increasingly cure our blindness. He does not speak of God's intervention contained in 2 Corinthians 4:4-6. Indeed, God must shine into our hearts if we are going to see at all. The 2 Peter 1:5-9 passage lists the virtues belonging to those who are not blind.
2. He places the authority of Scripture far higher than that of the saints.
3. Doing the Word and walking in obedience were more important to A'Kempis.
4. Answers may vary. He could have said, "Set your affections on things above" (vs. the invisible). Remember that Jesus Himself is a visible, corporeal being as He has both a human nature and a divine nature.

Section 2
1. Often learned men neglect their own souls. They are proud. Many of our universities do not teach in the fear of God and in humility before men. These virtues are not commended in much of academia, and therefore as Christians we must be very careful around the universities and the academy.
2. God expects that they do the Word.

Section 3
1. Jesus. He speaks in His Word—Old and New Testaments.
2. This is the life of the man who does all for the Glory of God, and not for self.
3. He won't look at what we have read, but what we have done. It won't be important how eloquently we have spoken, but how holy we have lived.

Section 4
1. Man is depraved and not to be trusted. He is pessimistic. Biblical texts affirming this: Rom. 3:1-15, Eph. 2:1-2, 2 Cor. 4:4-6
2. Answers may vary.

Section 5
1. The simple interpretation is usually the best, per A'Kempis.

Section 6
1. Proud and covetous men are never happy.
2. A worldly man does not resist his passions. The spiritual man does resist his passions and he has peace of heart. Yes, this is a contrast of a believer and an unbeliever.

Section 7
1. Answers may vary.

Section 8
1. It would be hard to find biblical precedent for this hesitancy. Jesus called his disciples "friends." David and Jonathan were friends.

Section 9
1. James 3:1
2. Answers may vary.

Section 10
1. No, the Bible is filled with exhortations to hospitality and entertaining the stranger and the widow. Guards: Speak to edify, watch and pray, and speak on spiritual matters.

Section 11
1. We are not free from passions and lusts and are therefore easily dejected. Answers may vary.
2. If we stand firm and fight, we can expect God's grace to help us. Yet, the Scriptures say it is still God who works in us both to will and to do of His good pleasure.
3. Breaking off bad habits. Resisting evil inclinations at the beginning. Fighting our passions and lusts. (Although he does not define or denote these passions and bad habits.)

Section 12
1. It compels a man to search his own heart. It also reminds him that he is a only a sojourner through this world and keeps him from getting too comfortable here. It helps us look forward to heaven.

Section 13
1. You are overcome by enduring patiently, seeking regular advice, and being on guard from the outset of temptation.
2. In times of temptation, great merit may be attained and our progress is tested. We can tell whether we are growing in our Christian lives by how well we overcome temptation.
3. Publius Ovidius Naso (43 BC-AD 17) was a Roman poet, also known in history as Ovid. He quotes this unbelieving Roman in a positive light, applying a principle the man used in the secular world to the Christian in the midst of temptation.
4. God disposes all things for the salvation of those whom He chooses. Here he affirms the sovereignty of God in election and acknowledges that God is sovereign over every trial and temptation that faces the believer.

Section 14
1. Because God is not our complete desire. We do not love God enough.
2. We are born with an inclination to sin.

Section 15
1. Yes. Love is the key good motive. Worldly motives include natural inclination, self-will, hope of reward, and self-interest.

Section 16
1. Because you are filled with faults and frailties too. Because God can bring good out of evil, and God can change others in due time.

Great Christian Classics: Four Essential Works of the Faith

Section 17
1. A habit is a monk's external robe, and the tonsure is the part of his hair left bare on the top.
2. Answers may vary. He seems to prefer people staying with the monastic community their entire lives.
3. Be servant-minded. Be humble. Be willing to be counted a fool for Christ. Do not gossip. Do not be idle.
4. He does not define the word "passions," so it is hard to determine whether he is condemning all earthly desires whatsoever. The Bible does not condemn married people having a passionate love for each other. In fact, this is encouraged in 1 Corinthians 7. The Bible teaches that we are to seek God first and foremost. But there is nothing wrong with seeking to make a living for the glory of God.

Section 18
1. Answers may vary. Apostle Paul, Polycarp, Justin Martyr, Origen, Tertullian, Augustine, etc.
2. Answers may vary. Hebrews 11 and the testimony of the Apostle Paul. Perhaps he read of the martyrs in Eusebius' *Ecclesiastical History*.
3. Generally, the word "perfect" speaks of a maturity—as we would speak of a "grown man." It does not refer to moral perfection.
4. At the outset of any of the ecclesiastical order, there was usually a strong discipline and vibrant spiritual fervency. By the 15th century, many of these orders had been around for hundreds of years and had grown lax in discipline. The student should research a little into what was happening during this pre-Reformational period.

Section 19
1. God determines what will happen. God disposes.
2. The monks participated in religious festivals. They had public devotions that were esteemed as more important than private devotions. They were to live more devoutly during these "holy seasons."

Section 20
1. Seneca was a Roman Stoic philosopher who lived around the time of Christ (4 BC-AD 65).
2. Answers may vary. It does seem that he draws more from a pagan philosopher than he does from the Bible. The Apostle Paul was constantly ministering to others. While it is true that it is easier to avoid temptation when we are in solitude, perhaps God would have us take some risks in order to take dominion, raise families, and edify the saints in the context of the Church.

Section 21
1. Contrition is sorrow over sin. Psalm 80:5, Psalm 51, etc.
2. A'Kempis thinks that men should always find cause for grief and tears. The world should always be bitter and grievous to us. The Bible teaches us that it is those who mourn who will laugh (Matt. 5). There is a place for mourning and a place for laughter.
3. Answers may vary. Jesus taught that hell fire would await the "workers of iniquity." Hell is a biblical doctrine. The idea of purgatory cannot be found in the Bible.

Section 22
1. Those who suffer for love of God.
2. The riches on earth are fleeting, uncertain, and even burdensome.
3. No. He plainly states that as long as we are in this body, we will have sin in our lives.

Section 23
1. Answers may vary.

Section 24
1. 1 John 1:9 tells us that confession does lead to cleansing however, it is God who is faithful and just to do this. Our confession and sadness do not do the cleansing. This is a thin distinction but an important one.
2. No. He speaks of purgation, but those in the fire appear to be the damned, the proud or the goats and tares.
3. He mentions the idea of "merit" in many places, as in "to merit to pass joyfully into the presence of God" (in Section 23). He speaks of "gathering the riches of eternal life." He expounds at length on the fears of purgatory in which a man will be "the more severely punished" if he doesn't deal with his sins on earth. Jesus does promise treasures in heaven to those who put their treasures there. Jesus also warns of hell fire. He tells us that it would be better for us to lose a hand or an eye on earth in our mortification of sin, than to lose everything in hell fire. But the motivation of love for God is basic to the Christian life (Deut. 6:4, John 21:20ff, 1 John 4:19-21, etc.) The Bible, however, does not speak of "meriting" heaven as A'Kempis does here. In the final paragraph of Section 23, he does refer to the motivation of love for God, but neglects the root of faith.
4. Yes. Ezekiel 18:21, Acts 26:20

Section 25
1. Just obey and do the will of God, and you won't need to worry about your salvation. He also admonishes us to "hope in the Lord."
2. Carthusians - The order of St. Bruno of Cologne founded in 1084. They were a strict order emphasizing silence and manual labor. Cistercians - The strict order of white monks founded by Robert of Molesme in 1098, emphasized manual labor.
3. Singing God's praises and being given over to spiritual things.
4. By enjoying God perfectly in all things.

BOOK TWO VOCABULARY 1
1. b
2. e
3. f
4. a
5. c
6. d

BOOK TWO VOCABULARY 2
1. d

2. f
3. a
4. e
5. g
6. b
7. c

BOOK TWO QUESTIONS

Section 1
1. Prepare your heart. Keep the Word of Christ. Put your whole trust in God. Direct worship and love to Him alone.
2. Christ suffered many things, including abandonment of friends. Christ had enemies and slanderers. Remember that if you suffer with Christ, you will reign with Him some day. His love makes it all worthwhile.
3. Selfish love of creatures. Relying on outward consolations and the kudos of men. Wholly immersing yourself in outward things.

Section 2
1. Confess your faults readily to others. Keep a clean conscience before God.

Section 3
1. He is not suspicious of others, but thinks the best of them. He exercises humble forbearance and focuses on his own affairs.

Section 4
1. Purity inspires affections and simplicity inspires purpose. Simplicity reaches out to God as the chief purpose in life. Purity discovers and enjoys God.
2. No human could possibly understand all things perfectly and comprehensively as God understands things (Rom. 11:33-35).

Section 5
1. Because we don't see things from the perspective of others. We are usually quick to excuse ourselves and cannot see our own faults very well.

Section 6
1. Preserve a quiet conscience. Care neither for praise or blame. Praise or blame won't change who you are at the core.

Section 7
1. A relationship of love and trust.

Section 8
1. Matthew 13:43-46
2. Answers may vary. The second reference is clearer than the first. It appears that the "losing of God's grace" would happen during dark days and difficult times in the Christian life—but it is not a loss of salvation.

Section 9
1. Laurence was deacon in the Roman church, martyred in 258. Sixtus was the bishop or elder of Rome who was also martyred at the same time. Historical records indicate that Laurence was martyred three days after Sixtus, and most, if not all, of his compatriots were martyred.
2. With humility. Without presumption. Be even more cautious and prepare for the tough times ahead.
3. Patiently endure, continue doing the will of God.
4. Yes, at least to every believer with which he was acquainted.

Section 10
1. Spiritual comfort.
2. Self-confidence, pride, and ingratitude.

Section 11
1. Loving Jesus for His own sake, not for the comfort we get out of it. Blessing Him still through our trials. A willingness to take up His cross and to suffer for Him.
2. Total self-denial.

Section 12
1. The way to hell and the way of the cross to heaven.
2. There is salvation in this way: protection, strength of mind, joy of spirit, perfection of holiness, and hope of eternal life.
3. Suffering for Christ. Daily self-denial.
4. When trouble seems sweet and acceptable to you in Christ. (When you count it all joy to fall into various trials.)
5. Answers may vary.

BOOK THREE VOCABULARY 1
1. c
2. e
3. f
4. d
5. a
6. b

BOOK THREE VOCABULARY 2
1. g
2. f
3. d
4. e
5. a
6. c
7. b

BOOK THREE QUESTIONS

Section 1
1. From His Word.

Section 2
1. Here is a development of how the Spirit of God works through the Word of God to bring spiritual understanding and application into the life: They instruct in the letter, but God opens the understanding. They teach commandments, but God helps us to apply them in our lives. They water the seed, but God produces the

increase. They warn in the Word, but God kindles the heart.
2. The word turns to condemnation. He is beaten with many stripes (Luke 12:47).

Section 3
1. Answers may vary. So far as it is a reflection of the words of Christ in the Bible, one can hardly argue with it.
2. That people will strive for earthly gain and yet be hardly motivated to seek the kingdom of God and lay up treasures in heaven. Christ is also more faithful than any earthly master.
3. Answer may vary. It demonstrates the close relationship that a believer has with Christ such that he talks with Him and receives Christ's words and personal, direct communication to his own heart.

Section 4
1. He doesn't condemn them as sinful. But they are too external and do not take Christ into the heart. Yes.
2. Of ourselves, we are nothing. Our good deeds do not make us anything more than sinners.

Section 5
1. A'Kempis adds: love is manly. Love is subject and obedient to superiors. Love is devoted and thankful to God. Love is neither soft nor light.
2. He calls God "above all" and the source of every good thing.

Section 6
1. Because he requires constant reassurance and is not able to walk through trials with a trusting and loving heart.
2. Veneration (or honoring the saints) was seen as an act of honoring God. Roman Catholic theologians distinguish between *latria* worship to God alone and *dulia* veneration given to saints and icons. Such a distinction is not to be found in Scripture, however. Hebrews 11 does recognize the faith of those who went before. But it would not commend an inappropriate hero-worship, the kissing of relics, or the bowing before a statue of a saint. Shadrach, Meshach, and Abednego would not bow before the statue of a king, and were persecuted for it.

Section 7
1. Pride. Refusal to listen to good counsel.
2. He condemns those who become too secure in times of peace (and presume on God) and who also become too dejected and fearful in times of trial.

Section 8
1. Dangerous, with many trials. He easily sinks into the depths without God's saving hand.

Section 9
1. They will never experience true joy. And they will be burdened and distressed by many things.
2. Answers may vary.

Section 10
1. By His creation, by His commands, and by His salvation in drawing us back to Himself.
2. Answers may vary.

Section 11
1. That there is some element of self-seeking in the life of the disciple, when he is acting for his own advantage rather than for the honor of Christ.
2. He acknowledges both good desires and bad desires. Although A'Kempis seems to confuse the use of the term from time to time, it does appear that he is referring to the "bad desires" or the flesh that wars against the Spirit here (see also Rom. 7:22ff).

Section 12
1. Remember that "purgatory" would be worse than anything you would suffer here. Everybody suffers. The men of this world will suffer in hell far worse for their focus on temporary pleasure.

Section 13
1. He refers to being "victorious over flesh and blood." This appears as a repudiation of the body (in the neoplatonic sense).
2. Christ points out that He Himself submitted to earthly authorities while He humbled Himself.
3. No. The Bible itself refers to us as "dust." Man's problem is not self-esteem—it is God-esteem. Man's problem is also pride.

Section 14
1. Absolutely not. We need God's hand from the beginning to the end of our salvation, for our justification, our sanctification, and our glorification.

Section 15
2. It is easy to confuse the Spirit with your spirit or some bad spirit.
3. Answers may vary. It seems that A'Kempis does not make this distinction.

Section 16
1. He seems to repudiate desires when it comes to temporal things like eating and drinking. That is, one should not desire these things. They are useful things to keep us alive, but they should not be desired. Our desire should be entirely for God and for heavenly things. Biblically, we should not be controlled by these earthly, temporal things, and we should not idolize them. But the Bible allows for one to desire food or drink as we do request that God provide us our daily bread. And we should be grateful for it and enjoy it.

Section 17
1. Because our names are written in the Book of Life.

Section 18
1. The way seemed darker in the Old Testament. Few cared to seek the eternal kingdom. The elect could not enter heaven before Christ died. We have Christ and His miracles and teaching, as our example, whereas the Old Testament believers did not.

Section 19
1. Yes. The disciple is complaining over his trials, and Christ is correcting his perceptions of this life of trial.
2. Our mind and habits should be trained to expect trials. Don't focus on the one who is persecuting you. Accept it gratefully from the hand of God. Remember, it is God who rewards you.

Section 20
1. He confesses being prone to discouragement, prone to fall, and weak in resisting his passions.
2. He doesn't want us to love the world, and he seems to be decrying the love of life. Again, A'Kempis is not always good about defining his use of the words "world" and "life." The Bible wants us hating our life in comparison to our love of God.

Section 21
1. Answers may vary. Song of Solomon is sometimes used as analogical language for our relationship to Christ.
2. We are fettered to the many evils that prevent us from free access to God.

Section 22
1. It seems that A'Kempis must maintain that all is the grace of God.
2. Those who realize their own poverty and vileness, the humble.

Section 23
1. Seek to do the will of others. None. (The Bible speaks of preferring one another but not doing the will of others.) Always choose to have less rather than more. None. Look always for the last place (Luke 14:10). Pray for the will of God to be fully carried out (Matthew 6:10).

Section 24
1. What other people say and do.

Section 25
1. Offering yourself with all your heart to the divine will. Not seeking your own desires.

Section 26
1. Answers may vary. Probably adulterous thoughts.
2. Desiring them too greatly. Letting these desires conquer you. You should participate only enough to sustain nature. Answers may vary. There does seem to be a role for "enjoying" your bread and wine in Scripture. Ecclesiastes 9:7, Isaiah 16:10.

Section 27
1. Don't let them hinder you or let them rob you of your freedom. Don't multiply earthly goods.

Section 28
1. You should already believe that nobody on earth could be worse than you. Their thoughts of you are incapable of making you better or worse.

Section 30
1. He seeks his comforts elsewhere, specifically from material things, before he even thinks about calling on God for help.
2. To keep us from being puffed up. Everything belongs to God and He has a right to take things from us anytime He wishes to. God wants us bringing forth much fruit to repentance.

Section 31
1. Evidently, it is the "contemplative life." But this is unrealistic and unbiblical because it does not reflect a biblical piety.

Section 32
1. Covetousness and curiosity, searching for ease.
2. Not to think too highly of self. Not to seek glory on earth.

Section 33
1. Being subject to our feelings. Losing a singleness of intention.

Section 34
1. He struggles with his flesh. He doesn't disdain the world enough.

Section 35
2. A dangerous life filled with many battles and surrounded by many enemies. There will be trials. Expect them.
3. Set your heart on Christ (faith). Be determined to suffer for Christ. Do not seek rest, but patiently endure.

Section 36
1. Trust in God. Do not fear men. Stay humble before God at all times.
2. Only so as to not scandalize the weaker brother.

Section 37
1. Jesus speaks of denying ourselves or disowning ourselves in Mark 8:34-38. We are to lose or give up our lives for Jesus and the Gospel.

Section 38
1. Freedom is self-control. Freedom is not letting anything have mastery over you (food, alcohol, etc.). Freedom is keeping one eye on heaven while you have one eye on earth. Freedom is using things in this world according to the laws of God.
2. Stay in prayer and consultation with God.

Section 39
1. He affirms that Christ will dispose our cause rightly in His time.

Section 40
1. Of himself, there is nothing that is good. Man is weak and unstable.
2. Answers may vary. Jews may have been known for seeking temporal honor and wealth.

Section 41
1. To be willingly despised and forsaken of men.

Section 42
1. Yes, he says this lack of grief is a virtue. However, we find in the Bible that Jesus wept at the death of his friend, Lazarus. For the Christian, grief should be contained.
2. Love for friends should be grounded in Christ. That is, our love for Christ should trump all other loves. He seems to discourage friendships as a form of weakness and a less than spiritual desire for comfort. One would have a hard time finding biblical warrant for that.

Section 43
1. By listening to Jesus rather than enquiring of men concerning "many things."

Section 44
1. It is an ignorance about things that would create more conflict than peace and love.

Section 45
1. Weak, unstable, untrustworthy, lying. Answers may vary.
2. Our life is all temptation and warfare.

Section 46
1. Don't be afraid to be despised. If you are deserving of the words, take them with humility of heart. If you are not deserving of the words, receive the abasement anyway as a good tonic to pride. Words will not harm a hair on your head. (However, they may harm your reputation.) Trust in God will free you from the fear of man. Remember, the judgment of men is nowhere near as accurate as God's judgment.

Section 47
1. Heaven and the joys that await us there.

Section 48
1. The beauties of heaven and the miseries of this earth.
2. Towards what you love.

Section 49
1. When the commands seem inconvenient or useless.
2. A'Kempis tells the reader to try to perform the will of the superior, inferior, or equal. The Bible does tell us to submit ourselves one to another. But this does not necessarily mean obedience in everything people tell us to do. It is listening with humility and following through with obedience to a word fitly spoken.

Section 50
1. "Nothing happens without your design and providence and without cause." He also acknowledges that every trial he meets, bitter blows or inflicting sorrows, is from the hand of God. Bitter blows, inflicting sorrows, etc.

Section 51
1. Divine contemplation and spiritual exercises. Biblically speaking, man's highest duty is to glorify God (1 Cor. 10:31), and we do this in and through physical things like eating, drinking, working, etc. A'Kempis seems to draw a dichotomy between the "spiritual" and the "physical."

Section 52
1. A'Kempis doesn't mention any form of "merit" in this chapter. If we come to God with a humble and contrite heart, we are received and forgiven on the basis of nothing we have done.

Section 53
1. The root of self-love.
2. The Bible says, "No man ever yet hated himself." (Eph. 5:29) What Jesus commends is denying oneself in that we put Jesus first in all things. We must love Him *more* than all else, including our own life.

Section 54
1. Nature is what lies in the natural man that receives not the things of God (1 Cor. 2:14). Grace is what is bestowed upon the regenerate man by the Spirit of God.
2. Nature likes honor and reverence, fears shame, loves ease and physical rest, and rejoices in earthly gain. Grace seeks to be profitable to others, embraces labor willingly, and delights in simple, humble things.

Section 55
1. He believes that man's reason is not entirely corrupted by the fall because it has the power of judging good and evil, and some power to accomplish good. Romans 3:1-14 and other passages teach just the opposite. Man cannot do good. Nevertheless, A'Kempis seems to contradict himself later by saying that he cannot do any good whatsoever short of the grace of God.

Section 56
1. If you will possess the blessed life, despise this present life. If you will be exalted in heaven, humble yourself on earth.

Section 57
1. "You are manly enough so long as you meet no opposition." Christ used this language with the Pharisees in Matthew 23. Romans 2:21 is also a similar example.
2. This is a man, who under great pressure and criticism, continues to respond cheerfully and does not allow it to confuse or discourage him. A mature man is one who can weather a storm without buckling.

Section 58
1. Which saints are greater than others and "merit" more than others. Why some people bear much heavier trials than others.
2. He believes that all good that any saint has ever done was a matter of predestination and grace. Thus, God's sovereignty is behind all those who work out their salvation with fear and trembling.

Section 59
1. God.

BOOK FOUR VOCABULARY 1
1. d
2. a
3. f

4. c
5. b
6. e

BOOK FOUR VOCABULARY 2
1. b
2. c
3. f
4. a
5. d
6. g
7. e

BOOK FOUR QUESTIONS

Section 1
1. He believes that we receive His holy body at the table, and we must partake of the table to partake of life everlasting. He does predicate it on the "worthy and devout" reception of the elements.
2. Noah worked 100 years to build an ark. Moses put together the Ark of the Covenant. Solomon spent seven years building the Temple. Kind David danced before the Ark with all his strength. He is ashamed that he can hardly spend thirty minutes preparing himself for the Lord's table.
3. He contrasts the fervor of those who honored the saints with the general lack of enthusiasm people exhibit towards the worship and honor of God. This argument in and of itself raises questions concerning the honoring of the saints. Are the traditions of men making the Law of God of no effect?
4. Carelessness in regard to the Lord's table. (Especially in that many took the table on a daily basis.)

Section 2
1. By contrasting ourselves with God Himself. God is holy; we are the worst of sinners. God gives us heavenly food despite our sinful selves.
2. The following statement would indicate such: "You are contained whole and entire under the appearance of a little bread and wine." The bread and the wine have now only the appearance of bread and wine.

Section 3
1. We quickly fall into sin and become lax and weak.
2. Apparently, he does not partake daily (as he is not prepared to do so).
3. Humble and grateful that Christ should condescend to him.

Section 4
1. No, only to those loved ones who communicate devoutly.
2. Great grace. Growing virtue. Faith confirmed. Hope strengthened. Charity fanned into flame. Many consolations. Encouragement.

Section 5
1. Answers may vary. Only the priest had the power to consecrate the Body of Christ. A priest acts in Christ's place. Symbols seem to play strongly in the priest's work.

Section 6
1. If he does not receive the Lord's table, he will miss out on Life. Yet, he risks taking it unworthily and incurring God's displeasure.
2. Answers may vary.

Section 7
1. Answers may vary. Much of this section provides a good summary of our fleshly ways and our life in the flesh, thus it provides cause for conviction, confession, and repentance. His reference to "sacred vigils" and "saying the office" would be unfamiliar to Protestants. Also, "No greater satisfaction for washing away sin than to offer yourself purely and entirely to God with the offering of the Body of Christ in Mass," has no basis in Scripture and would have been taken to task by men like Luther and Calvin.

Section 8
1. Give yourself entirely to Him. Luke 14:33, Mark 8:35

Section 9
1. By His blood.
2. Flawed. Needing Christ to make them acceptable to God.
3. It is the Lord's Table. Evidently, the disciple is a priest responsible for making this "offering." In earlier Christian history, you find the Church Fathers referring to the Lord's table as a sacrifice of thanksgiving. Later in the Roman Church, the table became a sacrifice of expiation and propitiation. Scripture does not refer to the table as a sacrifice. It is communion with the crucified Savior (1 Cor. 10:14-18).

Section 10
1. Anxiety and scruples.
2. A'Kempis speaks of confessing sin and taking the Lord's Supper here.
3. Several reasons are given. But prominent among them is the desire to wander from this relationship with God and to put off confession and communion so as to live in sin.

Section 11
1. We will not need this sacrament, because we will finally be face-to-face with our Savior and will enjoy fellowship for eternity with Him.
2. The example of the saints who have gone before us. The holy books, but especially the Holy Book (Scripture).
3. Be holy and pure. Keep a good conscience and humbly confess sin. Only speak good and profitable things.

Section 12
1. Purge out the old leaven. Think on your transgressions with bitterness of soul. Confess sins. Prepare your house for a visit with a precious One. Maintain a heart attitude of fear, reverence, and love.

Section 13
1. Christian nations are renowned and favored by God.

Section 14
1. He watches others overwhelmed by intense heart love, affection, and devotion; some will even weep at the table.
2. Pray for it. Pray that you will feel the tenderness of His love.

Section 15
1. Sometimes small things but usually things that you would never have thought were that significant.
2. Humble yourself. Die to yourself. Free yourself from inordinate love or dislike for any creature.

Section 16
1. He calls himself involved in great evil and vices. He is poor and naked, imploring God's mercy. A hungry beggar. This is a proper view of a regenerate man. At our best, we are unprofitable servants (Luke 17:10). We are wretched men indeed (Rom. 7).

Section 17
1. John the Baptist and Jesus' mother Mary.
2. A desire that all peoples and nations praise the Savior. A desire that all peoples would pray for the disciple.

Section 18
1. He warns us not to examine the Table too carefully and say too much about it. Appreciate the mystery of the Table. God in His wisdom has determined not to tell us too much of it. Simple faith is commended over a lofty intellect. What you cannot understand, commit to the security of an all-powerful God. These were wise words indeed.
2. Augustine and Anselm said, "I believe in order to know." This places A'Kempis in the order of Christian thought and takes him out of the realm of Greek thought, which has done so much damage to the Christian faith.

EXAM
Multiple Choice
1. B
2. A
3. D
4. C
5. A, B, D
6. C
7. B
8. C
9. A

True or False
1. True
2. True
3. True
4. False
5. True
6. False
7. True

Match
1. e
2. c
3. a
4. b
5. d

Short Answer
1. Intellectual men tend to be proud and they do not fear God.
2. Augustine of Hippo or Anselm of Canterbury (either okay).
3. According to A'Kempis, nothing happens without the design and providence of God. Nothing happens without cause.

THE INSTITUTES OF THE CHRISTIAN RELIGION

BOOK ONE
Chapter 1 Vocabulary 1
1. e
2. h
3. b
4. d
5. f
6. a
7. c
8. g

Chapter 1 Questions
1. Our personal gifts and blessings, which could not have come from ourselves, tell us about God, their source. Our unhappiness, ignorance, vanity, need, weakness, and general depravity, show that God is the source of all wisdom and goodness.
2. We cannot see our sin and smallness clearly when we compare ourselves to other sinners. It is only by knowing God in His purity and greatness that we can rightly assess ourselves.
3. In the last sentence of the chapter, Calvin indicates that he is going to talk about our knowledge of God before he talks about our knowledge of mankind.

Chapter 2 Vocabulary 1
1. b
2. a
3. d
4. e
5. f
6. c

Chapter 2 Questions
1. No, we cannot. Evidence of true knowledge is shown in a person's belief and practice. If a person truly knows God, he knows that God is worthy of his worship.
2. Scripture shows God to be the Creator and the Redeemer. Book One is titled "The Knowledge of God the Creator," and Book Two is titled "The Knowledge of

God the Redeemer, in Christ."
3. "By 'piety' I mean the blend of reverence and love to God which realizing His blessings inspire."
4. False. Calvin thinks it is impossible to find out the essence of God (he calls it "fruitless speculation"); rather, he seeks to show how God acts in God's relationship to mankind as revealed by Scripture and history.
5. "The result of our knowledge ought to be first, that we learn reverence and awe, and second, that we should be led under its guidance to ask for every good thing from Him, and when we receive it to give thanks to Him."
6. "So this is pure and true religion: it is confidence in God coupled with genuine fear. This fear comprises willing reverence and true worship as God has commanded."

Chapter 3 Vocabulary 1
1. c
2. a
3. b

Chapter 3 Questions
1. The existence of idol worship proves that the awareness of God is written on every heart.

Chapter 4 Vocabulary 1
1. h
2. n
3. g
4. i
5. b
6. d
7. m
8. j
9. l
10. c
11. k
12. e
13. a
14. f

Chapter 4 Questions
1. He describes as "foolish" and "stupid" those who are vain and proud and so end up substituting their own imaginations for true knowledge of God. He cites Romans 1 and Psalm 14. He is not talking about a lack of intelligence.
2. Yes, being a fool is a moral fault.

Chapter 5 Vocabulary 1
1. c
2. a
3. d
4. b

Chapter 5 Questions
1. The visible world reflects something of the character of the invisible God (Heb. 11:3). God's eternal power and divine nature are seen in what is made (Rom. 1:19-20).
2. Man's natural intellect is not enough to rightly interpret what the world shows of God. The eyes of our mind need to be enlightened by faith from God.
3. It is ingratitude to God to miss the revelation of Himself through His creation and to spoil the "seeds of divine knowledge" God planted in our minds.

Chapter 6 Vocabulary 1
1. b
2. c
3. a

Chapter 6 Questions
1. Scripture helps us see and interpret clearly the testimony of God in the created world.
2. Obedience. "Not only does a true and complete faith originate in obedience, but all sound knowledge does the same."

Chapter 7 Vocabulary 1
1. d
2. h
3. f
4. g
5. b
6. e
7. c
8. a

Chapter 7 Questions
1. Yes and no. Yes, "Scripture shows clear proof of being spoken by God, and consequently of containing His divine truth." But no, it does not convince people apart from the Spirit. "But although we may defend God's holy Word against all opponents, it does not follow that we can establish in their hearts the conviction which faith demands." "Scripture... does not stoop to be assessed by evidence and argument." "We do not ask for proof or evidence..."
2. The "hidden witness of the Spirit" convinces us that God is the Author of Scripture.
3. Because our belief in Scripture is not based on evidence, it requires us to "submit our intellect" to it. We do not verify that Scripture is true before we believe it. We accept the truth of Scripture like we accept a gift; its truth is not something we have achieved so it should not make us proud.

Chapter 9 Vocabulary 1
1. e
2. d
3. b
4. a
5. c

Chapter 9 Questions
1. We look to the Word of God. "The work of the Spirit promised to us is not to create new and unfamiliar revelations... but to seal on our minds the very doctrine which the Gospel recommends." "Any spirit which bypasses the truth of God's Word, and suggests any other doctrine, is rightly suspected of pride and deceit."

2. Answers may vary. The "circular reasoning" reaction is that of a person who wants to live their whole life by their own logic and reasoning. We should recognize that the Word and the Spirit are gifts to the Church, and God will use them to accomplish His purposes in us. We have to trust God to keep us on the path of truth.

Chapter 13 Vocabulary 1
1. d
2. f
3. h
4. b
5. e
6. a
7. c
8. g

Chapter 13 Questions
1. Jesus is called God in relation to us, and He is called the Son in relation to the Father.
2. He says that "God" generally refers to the whole Godhead: Father, Son, and Spirit. But when we are talking about the Father in relation to the Son or the Father in relation to the Spirit, we can use "God" to refer to the Father specifically (i.e. the Son of God and the Spirit of God).

Chapter 14 Vocabulary 1
1. e
2. a
3. b
4. d
5. c

Chapter 14 Questions
1. "...first, by never forgetting the glorious perfection God shows in his creatures and second by applying what he sees to himself, keeping it deep in his heart." First, we should be amazed by creation itself and attribute its glory to God. Second, we should be moved to faith, prayer, praise, and love, because we live in God's world and he cares for us.

Chapter 15 Vocabulary 1
1. e
2. c
3. d
4. a
5. g
6. b
7. f

Chapter 15 Questions
1. He is concerned not to attribute man's sinful nature to God's perfect creation. He wants to make sure we do not shift the blame for our sin to God.
2. Men have consciences—they fear eternal, spiritual punishment. But the body alone cannot be afraid of eternal, spiritual punishment. Therefore, men have eternal souls.
3. God sent His Son to earth to become a man who was called the Second Adam. He came to restore us to true humanness, which is in the image of God. Our salvation from sin makes us more human, not less human.
4. A soul has both an intellect and a will. Both were created good in Adam despite the fact that he willed to do the wrong thing. "Adam could have remained upright if he had chosen."

Chapter 16 Vocabulary 1
1. h
2. f
3. j
4. i
5. c
6. g
7. a
8. e
9. d
10. k
11. b

Chapter 16 Questions
1. Providence refers to God being not only the Creator but also the active Preserver and Governor of all events and persons in His creation.
2. Not only is God able to do anything He pleases, but also He actually does everything He pleases. His omnipotence is active, not passive.
3. Calvin would say that God is active not just in creating the world but also in sustaining it. There are no impersonal forces of nature.
4. Calvin would say that God is never distant from His creation even if He chooses not to perform what we would call a miracle.
5. General providence is God's control of the natural order of things, and special providence is God's control over specific people and events. Calvin says that belief in general providence is fine as long as we don't deny God's special providence. His main concern is to persuade the reader to believe in God's special providence.
6. If some things happen by chance, then God is not in control of all things. If God is not in control of all things, then we cannot hope in Him to protect and save us.

Chapter 17 Vocabulary 1
1. c
2. f
3. i
4. h
5. b
6. d
7. e
8. g
9. a

Chapter 17 Questions
1. Some of the examples that Calvin gives: The person who does not take medicine because he says God is in control

of his health. The person who does not pray because he says God knows everything and has determined everything anyway. The person who does not care for the poor because he says God provides for them. The person who does not thank someone for giving him a gift because he believes all gifts are ultimately from God.

2. He says, "In his heart a man plans his course, but the Lord determines his steps" (Prov. 16:9). Just because God determines his steps does not mean that man should not plan his course. And a man should plan his course all the while recognizing that God will ultimately determine his steps.

3. Lesser causes are the agents God uses in our lives for blessings or curses. He says we should notice these causes and respect them. Where we have received God's gifts through someone else, we should give thanks to God and to His agents.

4. We should be relieved and liberated from all worry, to know that God orchestrates all things and does not leave us at the mercies of chance or other men. We know He takes care of us down to the smallest detail, with more love than He takes care of the sparrows.

5. Answers may vary. This, too, should be a comfort. No one can get in the way of God's plan for us. God uses even the evil of men for His good purposes.

BOOK TWO

Chapter 1 Vocabulary 1
1. i
2. q
3. h
4. f
5. r
6. s
7. e
8. g
9. n
10. p
11. j
12. o
13. l
14. a
15. m
16. k
17. d
18. b
19. u
20. c
21. t

Chapter 1 Questions
1. Socrates
2. The philosophers meant that man should not be ignorant of the best things about mankind, the things that lead him to be proud of himself. Calvin said we should know 1) the purpose for which we were made and the wonderful qualities God gave us, and 2) the wretched state which we now are in, with its shame and corruption, and our inability to meet God's purpose.

3. A Pelagian believes that man is not stained with original sin and thus is able to choose right or wrong.

4. If we are sinful only because we followed a bad example, then we are also saved by following Christ's example. In that case, we can only be saved if we are able to follow His example well enough under our own power. Instead, Calvin argues, citing Paul, that Adam's sin condemned us as a whole race at once because we are all connected. As a result, we can be saved by being united with Christ. We are saved not by our ability to follow Him but by His righteous work.

5. "Sins" are evil acts and thoughts. "Sin" is our fallen nature. Just as a bad tree bears bad fruit, our sinful nature bears sinful acts. "Original sin" is the "hereditary corruption and depravity of our nature."

Chapter 2 Vocabulary 1
1. b
2. c
3. f
4. a
5. d
6. e

Chapter 2 Questions
1. His natural gifts are his will and intellect; his supernatural gifts are righteousness and faith, love of God and neighbor, and the study of righteousness and holiness.
2. 1) "Love of truth fades out before it reaches the goal and then falls away into vanity." 2) "It often fails to discern what sort of knowledge it should try to acquire."
3. Spiritual discernment consists of: 1) the knowledge of God, 2) the knowledge of His fatherly love towards us, in which our salvation consists, and 3) the way in which we can run our lives in tune with the law of God. Human reason, without the Spirit, cannot discern these things.

Chapter 3 Vocabulary 1
1. d
2. l
3. k
4. b
5. i
6. h
7. e
8. a
9. f
10. c
11. j
12. g

Chapter 3 Questions
1. Cataline was known as an evil person, and Camillus was known as a virtuous man. They are both evil. It is just that Camillus is better at hiding his evil vices under a "cloak of virtue."

2. Man sins freely because his sin is his own choice; he is not coerced by God. But man is bound to freely choose sin by his own corrupt nature. "Voluntary bondage" means that man chooses to be a slave to sin and that the will "imposes a necessity upon itself," and because it was still a free choice it is an inexcusable slavery.
3. "[T]here can be no doubt that by the good work begun he means the first step of conversion in the will. So God begins the good work in us by arousing in our hearts a desire, love and study of righteousness."
4. He wants to make sure man has no reason to boast about his own goodness to God. Even the good will to ask God for His favor comes from God. "Men must indeed be taught that God's favor is offered, without exception, to all who ask for it, but since only those who are inspired by God's grace do ask, every particle of praise must go to him."
5. Answers may vary. God converts people, efficaciously calling them to himself. He does not just give them the option to follow him but definitively changes their hearts and wills.

Chapter 6 Vocabulary 1
1. c
2. b
3. a

Chapter 6 Questions
1. You must believe in Christ and be ingrafted into the Body of Christ, the only begotten Son, in order to be counted as a son and call God your Father.

Chapter 7 Vocabulary 1
1. k
2. j
3. e
4. i
5. f
6. g
7. b
8. d
9. a
10. c
11. h

Chapter 7 Questions
1. "First, by displaying the righteousness of God, it rebukes everyone for his own unrighteousness, puts him on trial, convicts, and finally condemns him." In other words, the first use is to show sinners their need of Christ. "The second function of the Law is to control those who would have no concern for just and right behavior, unless there was fear of punishment." The second use is to be employed, for example, by civil authorities in restraining criminals. "The third function of the Law (which is the main one and most ultimately connected with its ultimate purpose) refers to believers in whose hearts God's Spirit already reigns... [The Law] is the best means for them to learn daily, with greater certainty, what the will of the Lord is which they long to follow." The third use is to show believers how to live.
2. Answers may vary. Calvin says the third use is the primary one. Perhaps this is because it is the only use of the law that would remain even if man had not sinned and will remain even in heaven.

Chapter 8 Vocabulary 1
1. j
2. c
3. d
4. b
5. f
6. g
7. e
8. a
9. h
10. i

Chapter 8 Questions
1. "To fill our hearts with love for himself and with hatred for sin, he has added promises and warnings." He wants love, manifesting itself in obedience to His Law.
2. No. God is entitled to our obedience since we belong to Him. The Law teaches us what pleases Him.
3. God's Law commands not just the outward obedience of the body, but also obedience of the soul.
4. Both make observing the Law a matter of loving God. They are also similar in that they both mention that obedience involves one's "heart" and "soul."

Chapter 9 Vocabulary 1
1. d
2. a
3. b
4. c

Chapter 9 Questions
1. In the Gospel we are forgiven and freely accepted by God, whereas the Law requires perfect obedience.
2. The Gospel has not ushered in a different plan of salvation from that of the Law—their goal is the same.
3. They differ "only by clarity of expression."

Chapter 12 Vocabulary 1
1. b
2. a
3. c

Chapter 12 Questions
1. He had to unite Himself to us in order to save us. He had to suffer and die to pay the price for our sin, and only a man can do that.
2. He had to unite us to God in order to save us—He had to be a Son of God to make us sons of God. He had to be able to conquer death, and only God can do that.

Chapter 14 Vocabulary 1
1. c
2. a
3. d

4. b

Chapter 14 Questions

No, Calvin is not saying that. The point of the illustration is that just as humans have a body and soul (and sometimes we refer to them as distinct even though they are both an integral part of the same person), so also Christ has a distinct human nature and divine nature, yet He is one person.

Chapter 16 Vocabulary 1
1. h
2. j
3. e
4. i
5. g
6. k
7. a
8. o
9. d
10. c
11. f
12. n
13. b
14. m
15. l

Chapter 16 Questions
1. So that we may be more grateful for the salvation God has provided us in Christ.
   Because He was dying in our place, He had to be "numbered as a transgressor"—that is, He had to be killed the way criminals were killed, not the way heroes are killed.
3. His resurrection restores to us righteousness and new life. Without it, our salvation would not be complete.
4. His reign began with His ascension into heaven—from there, "His power and reign have spread to the uttermost parts."
5. Christ is reigning with all authority on heaven and earth. He is the head of the Church and acts as our advocate to God the Father. He gives the Church gifts, He takes captives, He quickens us through His Spirit, He holds back enemies, and He is completing His Church.
6. Yes, Calvin says, "As he has entered it [heaven] in our flesh, it follows that in a way we are ourselves seated in heavenly places" (Eph. 2:5).
7. He is comforted because the only Judge has planned to share His honor with us. He also says we are the Body of Christ, and just as a head will not condemn its body, so there is no condemnation in Christ.

BOOK THREE

Chapter 1 Vocabulary 1
1. b
2. a

Chapter 1 Questions
1. Christ's death and resurrection benefit those who are united to Christ, who have Him as their "head."
2. The Spirit unites us to Christ, making us one with Him, so that we share His benefits and become His "brethren."

Chapter 2 Vocabulary 1
1. b
2. e
3. d
4. f
5. c
6. h
7. a
8. g

Chapter 2 Questions
1. Christ is the object of faith. Faith lays hold of Christ's work and His promises to us.
2. A prerequisite to faith is the conviction of God's truth. Faith involves a true knowledge of God, and that knowledge is found in His Word.
3. Faith is "a firm and sure knowledge of God's favour towards us, based on the truth of a free promise in Christ, revealed to our minds and sealed on our hearts by the Holy Spirit."
4. Calvin says assurance is an essential part of faith, but at the same time, we will never be completely free of distrust.

Chapter 3 Vocabulary 1
1. b
2. e
3. d
4. a
5. c

Chapter 3 Questions
1. Yes, Calvin says holiness is essential. This does not contradict justification by faith alone because a faith that is alive produces repentance, and repentance involves a change in one's life from sin to holiness.
2. It means to deny the desires of your sinful nature over and over again as if the old "you" was crucified in Christ once and for all.
3. When a person is born again, their sin is accounted to Christ and completely paid for in His death. The person is delivered from the bondage of sin once and for all. However, their sin remains for the rest of their life, and they must fight against it by the power of the Spirit. For the rest of their life, they must be purified from sin and guilt.

Chapter 6 Vocabulary 1
1. c
2. d
3. b
4. e
5. a

Chapter 6 Questions

1. It is a knowledge that has learned to put off the "old self" and put on Christ, so it is a way of living as a Christian.
2. Calvin says it is not possible to study God or right beliefs without following Christ. This is because doctrine is not just grasped by the intellect, but the whole goal is a fruitful life. Nothing is really learned if it doesn't change your life. Religion is not just something you think. It is not just between your ears, it extends to your fingertips.

Chapter 7 Vocabulary 1
1. c
2. d
3. a
4. e
5. b

Chapter 7 Questions
1. They made reason the sole ruler of man.
2. He is to seek the Lord's will and glory by obeying God's commandments, both of which include serving others.
3. If he denies himself, he will be serving the Church with whatever God has given him. Calvin says that no member of the Church exists for his own benefit, but for the building up of the whole Church.

Chapter 8 Vocabulary 1
1. b
2. c
3. e
4. a
5. d

Chapter 8 Questions
1. David was a great man, but even he needed God to show him his weakness by hiding His face from him. Calvin says believers need to experience suffering because it demonstrates our weakness, removes our arrogance, and causes us to turn to God for mercy.
2. Since God gives the strength to endure through tribulation and you could not endure it without Him at your side, this experience is "proof" that God gives what He promises.
3. Calvin says, "We don't all suffer from the same disease, so we don't all need the same cure." Some Christians do not care for the world's approval, but they themselves are not sure of their salvation so they need to be shown that they are fully accepted in Christ. Other Christians desire to be accepted by the world, and they need to have that stripped away so that they will seek acceptance from God alone.
4. First, we should realize that we deserve them and more as punishment for our sins. Second, we should realize that God is giving trials to us because He wants to save us. The latter is the most important part of our response.

Chapter 9 Vocabulary 1
1. c
2. f
3. g
4. a
5. d
6. b
7. e

Chapter 9 Questions
1. We should recognize that this world is a fleeting shadow compared to what God has in store for us in eternity. We should despise wealth and other earthly blessings compared to the value of our future joy with God.
2. If a person despises the world in a way that is ungrateful to God for giving it to him, that is sin. Even though this world's blessings are fleeting, they are still blessings, and they genuinely show us the goodness of God.

Chapter 10 Vocabulary 1
1. c
2. a
3. d
4. b

Chapter 10 Questions
1. We are to use them "as they are intended" by God.
2. It says that God is unnecessarily generous. He is not only the supreme standard of truth and righteousness but also of beauty.
3. Yes, in one word, the test is gratitude: Do we recognize that "the aim of creation is to teach us to know the Creator and feel gratitude for his generosity"? Not enjoying His creation is a form of ingratitude. Lusting after something in His creation is also a form of ingratitude. Both of these errors ignore the God who is giver.

Chapter 11 Vocabulary 1
1. c
2. a
3. b

Chapter 11 Questions
1. Yes, this is the definition of justification. Calvin says this can happen either by works or by faith, but for us sinners, it only happens by faith.
2. We are saved by Christ, through faith. Faith doesn't save us in itself because it isn't worth anything. Christ, our righteousness, is given to us and is received by faith in Him. We use the term "justification by faith" as a brief way to say this, but it should be remembered that it does not mean that our belief in God makes us righteous. Only God saves.
3. The difference is that in imputation, the righteousness is the obedience of Christ, and we are covered by it since we are united to Him. In the case of the influence theory, God affects us, but the righteousness that saves us is in ourselves. Calvin gives three passages of Scripture that support the idea of justification by imputation.

Chapter 12 Vocabulary 1
1. c
2. b
3. a

Chapter 12 Questions
1. Book I, Chapter 1 said that we need a knowledge of God to know ourselves truly. This chapter is reiterating that theme: it says that our lack of righteousness is not clearly seen unless we consider how righteous and pure God is and what it is to be judged by His standard.

Chapter 13 Vocabulary 1
1. b
2. a

Chapter 13 Questions
1. We are created by God, so we are never independent of Him. Our entire existence is defined by our relationship to Him, so it is impossible for a person to look at God and be ambivalent. Either a person is at peace with God or they are at war with God—but they cannot escape having a relationship with Him. Answers may vary.

Chapter 14 Vocabulary 1
1. c
2. a
3. d
4. e
5. b

Chapter 14 Questions
1. Though these gifts are given by God, they are exercised out of wrong motives and not out of a desire to serve God.
2. We should view our good works as gifts from God. They are never the basis of our standing before God, but they are part of God's work in saving us. Our good works should encourage us because they are proof that God is living in us and that He loves us.

Chapter 16 Vocabulary 1
1. a
2. c
3. b

Chapter 16 Questions
1. We are justified by being united to Christ in His righteousness, and we cannot be united to Christ without being given both faith and works. So works don't justify us, but we cannot be justified without works.

Chapter 17 Vocabulary 1
1. b
2. d
3. e
4. a
5. c

Chapter 17 Questions
1. Yes. Our works are imperfect in and of themselves, but they can be "imputed for righteousness" because they are perfected by Christ in the same way the justified person is clothed in Christ's righteousness.

Chapter 18 Vocabulary 1
1. c
2. a
3. d
4. b

Chapter 18 Questions
1. The three parts of Christian freedom are: 1) that we must not attempt to obtain righteousness from obedience to the Law but only from Christ; 2) that we obey the Law because we truly want to; and 3) that we are "not bound to observe outward regulations concerning unimportant matters." The first part of Christian freedom is very similar to the first use of the Law, that the Law shows us our unrighteousness and our need for Christ. The second and third parts of Christian freedom are related to the third use of the Law, that the Law tells Christians how to live, and we do not need to add unnecessary regulations on top of the Law. (The second use of the Law—"to control those who would have no concern for just and right behavior, unless there was fear of punishment"— is not related to the subject of Christian freedom because it applies to unbelievers who are not freed by Christ to obey the Law voluntarily.)

Chapter 20 Vocabulary 1
1. d
2. c
3. b
4. a

Chapter 20 Questions
1. Praying spurs on our faith, gives God the honor for the blessings we receive when we ask, and keeps us from trying to hide things from God.
2. If a person isn't aware that he needs anything from God, then he is not likely to pray even if he trusts God. If a person knows that he needs help but does not have confidence that God will answer his prayer, he is also not likely to pray. Even in the best of times, we need God's help, and even in the worst of times, we can trust that He will hear our prayer.
3. Answers may vary.

Chapter 21 Vocabulary 1
1. c
2. a
3. d
4. b

Chapter 21 Questions
1. He has written previously about salvation by God's grace and not by our works. Romans 11:5-6 identifies salvation by grace with being chosen by God. So it says that either God chooses whom He saves, or else salvation is by works. We already know salvation is not by our works, so we must accept God's sovereignty over our salvation.
2. He is exhorting us to look to Scripture to understand this doctrine, but he is warning us not to speculate about God's will and wisdom beyond what Scripture says.

Great Christian Classics: Four Essential Works of the Faith   345

Chapter 22 Vocabulary 1
1. d
2. a
3. b
4. c

Chapter 22 Questions
1. Calvin's main concern is the question: Who gets the glory for our salvation? He says that if there is anything in us that deserves salvation or makes us better than other men, then the glory would be ours, not God's. Therefore, for the glory to be God's, God must be completely free to save whom He will without regard to anything in us.
2. Answers may vary. Our culture is humanistic: it tries to make man sovereign over everything. It tries to turn the virtue of freedom into something all men deserve rather than something that is given by God, and in doing so, it actually leaves people in slavery to themselves and others.

Chapter 24 Vocabulary 1
1. b
2. e
3. d
4. a
5. f
6. c

Chapter 24 Questions
1. Calvin says we must look to Christ, and not to ourselves, to have assurance of salvation since we were not saved by anything in ourselves. Look to Christ, and believe His promises.
2. Since it was God that drew us to Himself in the first place and gave us faith, He will not let go of us (Phil 1:6; John 6:37-39; John 10:27-29).

Chapter 25 Vocabulary 1
1. b
2. d
3. a
4. c

Chapter 25 Questions
1. Christ was resurrected from the dead, not just as a spirit but in a glorified body as well. He was the "firstfruits" (1 Cor. 15:23) and we will follow Him in His resurrection because we are united to Him—He cannot be separated from His Church.

BOOK FOUR

Chapter 1 Vocabulary 1
1. c
2. e
3. d
4. b
5. i
6. j
7. g
8. a
9. h
10. f

Chapter 1 Questions
1. The point of both analogies is that there is no spiritual life outside of the Church. Like a mother, the Church is necessary for life. Like Israel, the Church is the only people of God, whom He loves. "Abandoning the Church is always fatal."
2. Yes, they can. Either they "seem all right" on the outside, or else they are "tolerated for a while."
3. Augustine says there are "very many wolves inside" the Church. Calvin's "loving assessment" is that we take people's profession of faith at face value. Thus if they confess Christ in Word and life and share in the sacraments, we should think them to be one of the sheep with us, and we should not question their salvation. It is more essential that we know if our church body is part of the true Church—that is more important than judging if someone else is elect or not.
4. Calvin gives two marks of the Church: the Word and the sacraments. "Wherever the Word of God is sincerely preached and listened to and wherever the sacraments are administered according to Christ's institution, we can be sure the Church of God exists."
5. The Church is "chosen and set apart" by Christ to be his "bride" and "body." A person who revolts from the Church while trying to keep a relationship with Christ is like a person who rejects their mother while wanting favor from their father who loves his wife.
6. Answers may vary.

Chapter 2 Vocabulary 1
1. c
2. g
3. b
4. f
5. d
6. a
7. e

Chapter 2 Questions
1. He is not revolting from the Church because the Church of Rome did not exhibit the marks of the Church: faithful preaching of the Word and right observance of the sacraments.
2. He first asks, rhetorically, why the papists don't talk about areas such as Egypt, where the succession was broken, or Greece, where the succession was unbroken but they turned away from Rome. Then, he says it is more important for succeeding generations not to turn away from Christ: "The pretence of succession is futile, if succeeding generations do not keep the truth of Christ (which was handed down by their fathers) safe and whole, continuing to live by it."

Chapter 3 Vocabulary 1
1. d
2. c

3. a
4. b

Chapter 3 Questions
1. God condescends to us and to the world by using men to represent Him. It also teaches us humility to obey ordinary men. Lastly, it binds us together as the Church to have the essential doctrine of salvation administered from men to men.
2. He gave us Church leaders: apostles, prophets, evangelists, pastors, and teachers (Eph. 4).

Chapter 12 Vocabulary 1
1. d
2. e
3. b
4. a
5. c

Chapter 12 Questions
1. 1) Private rebuke, 2) rebuke with witnesses, 3) correction by the body of elders, and 4) banishment from the company of believers. These are all found in Matthew 18.
2. For the honor of God. A "Christian" carries Christ's name, and that name should not be taken in vain. For the good of the Church. Regular contact with the wicked may lead good people astray. For the good of the person being disciplined. The discipline may cause them to repent and turn back to God. God may use it to save them.

Chapter 14 Vocabulary 1
1. c
2. d
3. b
4. e
5. a

Chapter 14 Questions
1. The sacraments are physical signs of God's promises to His covenant people. The sacraments are "visible words," presenting God's promises to us in touchable form.
2. Like a seal on a diploma, the sacraments put something into effect. They do present information to us about God's promises, but they also specifically apply the promises to you, and you really receive them in the sacramental ritual.

Chapter 15 Vocabulary 1
1. c
2. d
3. a
4. e
5. b

Chapter 15 Questions
1. 1) Cleansing from sin by Christ's blood, 2) being buried with Christ and raised in newness of life, and 3) assurance of union with Christ.
2. He says we should remember our baptism in order to be assured that our sins are forgiven. This is not putting our confidence in baptism, it is putting our confidence in Christ since the cleansing with Christ's blood is pictured and applied in baptism. Also, Calvin echoes Paul, reminding us that in baptism we died to sin and live for Christ—so we should remember our baptism in order to remember who we are to live for.

Chapter 16 Vocabulary 1
1. g
2. c
3. f
4. e
5. a
6. d
7. b

Chapter 16 Questions
8. He would be a God to them and to their seed. He would forgive their sins, and putting to death their flesh, He would give them new birth. He would also give them life and every blessing, including eternal life. These are the same promises as those Calvin has already identified with baptism.
9. He asks if the promises in the New Covenant are less than those of the Old Covenant. His answer is no: "We cannot imagine that Christ, by his coming, diminished the Father's grace... Surely we have to say that it [the Father's love] cannot be more restricted and less obvious than under the dark shadows of the Law." Therefore, God has not held back His promises from our children in the New Covenant; we are to raise them in God's family and not outside it.

Chapter 17 Vocabulary 1
1. b
2. d
3. a
4. c

Chapter 17 Questions
1. "The chief object of the sacrament is to seal and confirm his promise by which he testifies that his flesh is our food and his blood is our drink, feeding us to eternal life."
2. An empty sign is merely a reminder of Christ's death, and to partake of an empty sign is just to believe the eating itself doesn't matter. But here, Calvin insists that in the sign God also fulfills what He has promised when it is received with genuine faith and heartfelt gratitude. "If by the breaking of the bread, the Lord truly represents the partaking of his body, there can be no doubt that He imparts the reality too. We must always remember that the truth of the thing signified is also present."

EXAM
Multiple Choice
1. C
2. C
3. D
4. B

Great Christian Classics: Four Essential Works of the Faith

5. A
6. D
7. C
8. D
9. A
10. B
11. C
12. D
13. B

Fill in the Blank
1. First Use: A Mirror to show us our sinfulness; Second Use: To restrain the wickedness of men; Third Use: To act as a guide of righteousness for the believer
2. One: Prophet; Two: Priest; Three: King
3. One: Preaching of the Word; Two: Administration of the Sacraments

Short Answer
1. God is active governor and preserver of all events and persons in His creation.
2. Calvin teaches that justification and sanctification are distinct in their nature but always accompany one another and are inseparably linked.
3. Calvin argues that the sign of circumcision and baptism are related and that infants are included in the covenant promises of the New Testament just as they were in the Old Testament. Therefore, they are to be baptized.
4. Calvin summarizes the moral law by stating that the Ten Commandments teaches us to love God and love our neighbor.

Matching
1. e
2. a
3. b
4. c
5. d

THE PILGRIM'S PROGRESS

BOOK ONE

CHAPTER 1

Vocabulary
1. c
2. e
3. a
4. b
5. d

Questions
1. An allegory is a work in which the characters and events are to be understood as representing other things and symbolically expressing a deeper, often spiritual, moral, or political meaning. This story is a collection of characters and events all of which are intended to present a spiritual reality—the story of the Christian life.
2. His motivations were to be rid of his burden, to escape from the judgment coming upon the City of Destruction, and to gain eternal life and a place in heaven.
3. One thinks of Lot who flees from Sodom and Gomorrah. Also, Paul commands a separation from the world in 2 Corinthians 6:17. James speaks of those who are friends of the world as being enemies of God. There is a separation from the world required of true Christians.
4. His burden is sin. Nobody else in the City of Destruction senses this burden because they have not been convicted of their need for repentance. Yet they have sinned and fallen short of the glory of God. Their hearts are hardened, and they will not listen.
5. They were reluctant to join him because they did not want to leave all their worldly comforts and pleasures for the hard road to heaven. They were also hardened to his words. Families in the book of Acts (as in Lydia's, Cornelius', and the Jailer at Philippi's) were more than willing to join together in journeying to the Celestial City. It appears normative in Scripture that families participate in this journey.
6. Obstinate represents someone who stubbornly holds on to his worldly comforts and will not be dissuaded by promises of anything better because he refuses to believe that there is anything better. Pliable represents someone who is receptive but is easily led and pulled in every direction. He is always curious to hear some new thing, but his commitment is shallow. He also represents those who are attracted by the promise of good things at the end of the journey.
7. Christian's reaction differs in that he does not give up all hope and return to the City of Destruction. Instead, he calls for help and gets out on the side nearest the Wicket Gate—rather than returning to the City of Destruction.
8. Man does not need to go to the Cross for salvation but can find it in his own works. He is justified by the works of the law. Bunyan refers to the Roman Catholic church's position outlined at the Council of Trent. It is that form of religion that finds oneself to be "good enough for heaven," meriting heaven by a system of good works.
9. **a. Christian**: Christian is a man who is weighed down by his burden of sin after reading this book and feels convicted about it. He sincerely desires salvation and will do anything to rid himself of the burden on his back. He looks forward to the incorruptible inheritance in Christ's Kingdom and so forsakes everything to find eternal life in Christ. Christian symbolizes any human who has been convicted by sin and is now traveling down the road to heaven to rid himself of his burden. **b. Evangelist**: Evangelist is a wonderful guide to Christian throughout the journey. He returns as Christian's guide when Christian finds himself in trouble. He gives Christian wise advice to keep him on the straight and narrow way. Evangelist symbolizes a pastor—a shepherd of sheep—by the way he shepherds Christian through difficult situations and gives him good advice. **c. Obstinate**:

Obstinate is a neighbor of Christian's from the City of Destruction who runs after Christian when Christian runs away from the city. He tries to persuade Christian to come back but will not listen to Christian's invitation to come along. Obstinate is too consumed with the worldly pleasures and comforts. He can not bear to leave all these behind and go on an "unknown" road. He symbolizes a materialist, one who idolizes materials. **d. Pliable:** Pliable is another neighbor of Christian's who runs after him to bring him back. He joins the journey for a time, allured by the promises of what lies at the end of the journey. He knows no burden and is unwilling to accept hardship. He is entirely unprepared to encounter the obstacles and impediments along the trail. He is easily discouraged and abandons the journey after just a short while. **e. Help:** Help appears as a believer (probably not a pastor), but one who is familiar with the way through discouragements that easily afflict immature believers or those who are seeking the way. **f. Mr. Worldly Wiseman:** Worldly is a man who works hard to keep people from thinking about their sinful condition. He recommends a man named Legality, a man of "high morals" who has set for himself a system of morality that he pretends to keep. These are men who abandon the high standards of the Laws of God and work hard to keep a man from ever being burdened by the guilt of his own sins. They are psychiatrists, psychotherapists, cultural leaders, all humanists who insist on their own system of ethics.

CHAPTER 2

Vocabulary
1. d
2. c
3. e
4. b
5. a

Questions
1. He is one who shows things to Christian that will be profitable to him for his journey. He must be a teacher in the Church.
2. The man pictured in the hallway is Jesus.
3. The purpose of the Law is to convict a man of his sin, but it is God's grace that cleanses and washes him of that sin.
4. Patience portrays a man of godly character because he is willing to wait for the rewards that God has promised him. He is not satisfied with the things of the world but rather looks forward to a heavenly prize. Passion portrays a man of the world because he is not willing to wait for the rewards that God has promised him. He wants his worldly treasures and seeks happiness in them now, rather than placing his hopes in eternity.
5. Answers may vary. Through seemingly unbeatable odds, this man is willing to take on a company of soldiers, and he will win glory. It encourages us to not give up easily but to fight against all odds in the journey to heaven.
6. The man in the iron cage is hopelessly lost. He has no hope that he will ever be forgiven. In the illustration of the oil and water, it is the Spirit of God that continues to pour oil upon the flames, making it impossible for the devil to extinguish the spiritual life in the Christian's soul. Conclusion: Bunyan calls this man a professor but does not call this man regenerate. Therefore, he does not believe that you can lose your salvation.

CHAPTER 3

Vocabulary
1. c
2. d
3. b
4. e
5. a

Questions
1. Christian's burden of sin was removed. He is provided with white clothes and a scroll. This is the only visit recorded in the story.
2. The roll represents our assurance of eternal life and our acceptance into heaven.
3. Christian finds these men slumbering by the way with iron shackles on their legs. The shackles represent their sins, which they hardly notice. They are hardened to their sin and are like those who sleep when there is a battle waging. They have no motivation to escape the impending danger because their eyes are blinded to their sin.
4. Formalist and Hypocrisy are two men from the city of Vain Glory, who climb over the wall into the way. They are professing Christians, but their religion is all external. Their lives do not reflect their testimony, and hence they are hypocrites through and through. Their worship on Sunday is all in form, and there is no true heart of love and fear for God there. When it comes to impending difficulties and trials, these men will instinctively take the easy way out. In the end, it will lead to their destruction. Religion for them must be convenient, and require little sacrifice on their part—certainly no mortification of sin, confrontation, confession, and hard repentance. Churches are forever trying to make things convenient and easy in their advertising, their evangelism, their programs, and their preaching. And these men are the first to sign up for such outward religion. In the end, they meet their end by wandering from the path.
5. Answers may vary. Many heresies have dogged the Christian Church since the beginning. Thousands of denominations take different perspectives on major issues and minor issues. They cannot all be right. Jesus said, "Narrow is the gate, and the way that leads to life."
6. Because trials like Hill Difficulty are there to try our faith and make it stronger. It is there to test us to make sure our faith is really genuine and to sanctify us. We will be continually sanctified even after we are saved because faith without works is dead. Faith and works in a biblical construct are distinct but not separate (James 2).

Great Christian Classics: Four Essential Works of the Faith

7. Timorous and Mistrust turn back because of the lions in front of the Palace Beautiful. The character qualities they manifest are fear, doubt, cowardice, and lack of faith.
8. We are not to rest in the midst of difficulty. Oftentimes, we are tempted to "take a break" because we think that we deserve a rest in the battle with the world, the flesh, and the devil. Christian rested in the midst of difficulty and consequently left his Roll at the arbor. The Roll is the certificate certifying acceptance into the kingdom. It was his assurance.
9. A place of rest and refreshment for the weary pilgrims. There is good fellowship with the saints. This is a Church, or an assembly of God's people.
10. Evidently, the lions test the faith of those that would enter the Church. This is a Church that is not so easily joined. Even the watchman seems a little suspicious of the visitors. Watchmen are always concerned about charlatans, wolves, divisive folk, etc. that would harm the body of Christ in a local assembly. This is not your typical church growth effort.
11. Watchful is an elder who is called to be ever alert and watchful over the Church, to guard the body from grievous wolves. He encourages Christian past the lions, giving him confidence and reassurance.
12. They are virgins of the place who are there to encourage and give strength to the pilgrims for their journeys. Yes. They are sisters in Christ who provide hospitality in the body, which is one of the most important one-anothers God wants us to engage in, being part of the Church.
13. The things of this earth are growing dim in his estimation. His thoughts fill with detestation and sadness towards men like Formalist, Hypocrisy, Sloth, Presumption, etc. who are still drawn to the things of the world. He says that he might have looked back on it earlier as a place to be desired, but now he desires a more heavenly, glorious, and eternal resting place.
14. They gave him armor to help him on his journey, and they gave him encouraging stories concerning those who fought the good fight in ages past (Jael, Gideon, David). With these stories they provided him great encouragement, proving for him that nothing is impossible with God. Indeed, God protects us even when it seems as though we face unbeatable odds.

CHAPTER 4

Vocabulary
1. d
2. a
3. e
4. c
5. b

Questions
1. Apollyon is satan or the devil, the prince of the power of the air, the spirit that works in the children of disobedience (Eph. 2:2).
2. By insisting that he is the rightful king over Christian and calling him a traitor. By claiming that Christ is a more severe master than Apollyon. By threatening persecution and death. By pointing out that Christian has been unfaithful to Christ.
3. Answers may vary. This is a serious, life and death struggle for Christian in the valley.
4. The Valley of Humiliation is a fairly pleasant walk for most of the distance except for a major run-in with Apollyon. The Valley of the Shadow of Death is a long, arduous, treacherous, and torturous route.
5. He sees no other way to get to his desired destination. He is focused and will not be deterred. He is on his way to the Celestial City.
6. A very narrow path with harrowing ditches on either side. Frightening demons that discourage, tempt, and assault him throughout. Self doubts concerning his own thoughts.
7. The reminder that others had gone through this valley besides himself, and they had made it intact. The reminder that God would be with him throughout the valley. He hoped he could catch up with one who was walking through the valley now. Prayer and the repeating of biblical passages and promises.
8. These giants had both persecuted Christians over the years in Europe. Many Christians fell to the tyrannical, evil despots of State and Centralized Church Power. Few Christians in America may be dying for their faith today at the hands of the Catholic Popes or the State, but paganism is alive and well in China, Iran, Indonesia, and even Sweden.

CHAPTER 5

Vocabulary
1. d
2. a
3. b
4. c
5. e

Questions
1. He almost immediately trips and falls.
2. Wanton is a woman who tempts a man to sexual sin. These women are everywhere. They hover in the minds of many young men, and for years they are hardly rid of them. These Wanton characters distract young men from the fear of God, the pure worship of God, and the way of righteousness.
3. Negative. They tempt Faithful to think that by fulfilling the law he might obtain a right standing with God. Of course, this is a pipe dream. In the end, the law without Christ provides nothing but cruel, heartless beatings upon the soul. The law can provide no forgiveness, no atonement—only condemnation. And this is why Faithful received such a beating.
4. Shame defines what is right and true by whether it will produce the most wealth and power for the person who holds to it. He scoffs at those who seek first the Kingdom

of God. He notes that most rich and powerful people are not men of faith. Therefore, he concludes that there must not be much truth in "religion" or at least the Christian faith. He is a proud man and despises people who are convicted of their sins and humble themselves to ask forgiveness of God or their neighbor.

5. He believes that talking about things is most profitable. He loves the theoretical and the theological discussions. But he sees very little value in applying the Word of God in real life. He disagrees with James. "Be ye doers of the word and not hearers only." He separates knowledge and life application. He separates faith and works.

CHAPTER 6

Vocabulary
1. e
2. a
3. d
4. b
5. c

Questions
1. Encouragement. He encourages them to keep plodding on, that the reward is waiting for them, and not to grow weary in well doing. Then he promises that they will continue to go through hardship and persecutions in this world. This is an excellent example of pastoral care. Pastors should warn their congregants of the difficulties they will face and prepare them to take those difficulties on as true men of God. Paul instructed Timothy of these things in his epistles. And this is what we find in Galatians 6, Ephesians 6, and other passages throughout Scripture.
2. "World" is used in different ways in the Bible. There is a "World" that God loved and He came to save. It is the world of birds, families, dirt, stars, and governments. There is a "world" that we are not to love. "Love not the world neither the things that are in the world." This world is defined by John as "the lust of the flesh, the lust of the eyes, and the pride of life." It is the world where every imagination against Christ is considered, exalted, and lived out (2 Cor. 10:5). Vanity Fair is the world in the second sense.
3. He speaks of the wares of Rome as greatly popular in Vanity Fair—in fact the most popular among the people of the world (at least in Europe at that time.) It is no doubt the teachings and practices of the Roman Catholic Church.
4. Each culture has its own cultural practices that do not reflect the ways of God. Each culture has their own unique sins, ideas, and practices that do not conform to the Word of God.
5. Sin. The wrong priorities in life. When people prefer money to serving Christ, and they prioritize economic gain over loving their children, discipling their families for Christ, engaging in worship—then they are buying the wares of Vanity Fair. Bunyan is not decrying the ownership of gold, silver, houses, or lands. It is the system of life, the priorities, and the commitments of the world that he rejects.
6. They were clothed differently. They appeared different to the people around them. (Bunyan speaks of outward behavior, not necessarily clothing. They spoke differently. Their language obviously reflected their priorities in life as they spoke of Christ, God's glory, the church, love of the brethren, the worship of God, and the things that mean nothing to unbelievers. They did not get excited about the ideas, the priorities, and materials sold at the fair.
7. For the same reason that Abel was persecuted by Cain, Joseph was persecuted by his brothers, and Christ was put to death. The contrast of the believer and unbeliever is sharp. This either convicts the unbeliever of his sin and draws him to Christ, or it hardens him in his sin. The unbeliever assumes that he is the standard of all that is righteous. If then the believer marks a sharp contrast to him, then he must be the epitome of evil. In short, the unbeliever is consumed with white-hot hatred and envy against believers in these circumstances.
8. Answers may vary. Most of the satire is contained in the names of the characters involved. The characters think themselves as those with the highest virtue. The hypocrisy is thick.
9. First, he points out that the ideas upheld by Vanity Fair are diametrically opposed to the Word of God. Faithful presupposes the Word of God as the absolute standard for truth. Secondly, he states his opposition to any worship not agreeable to the Word of God (a light version of the Reformed "Regulative Principle of Worship.") Thirdly, he states his conviction that the ruler of the town should go to hell. Faithful doesn't mince words—there is no compromise in his faithful testimony.
10. Because God would have it that way. Bunyan acknowledges the absolute sovereignty of God over every king, every judge, and every persecutor of the Christian.

CHAPTER 7

Vocabulary
1. b
2. c
3. a
4. d
5. e

Questions
1. Answers may vary. They are men from the town of Fair-Speech. These are good-looking, smooth-talking men who are usually pretty impressive to the world around them. They hate to speak of sin, repentance, and trials. They present messages on "Worldly Success," "Ten Steps to a Happy Life," and "How to Live Your Best Life Now." They seem to want to give up any and all standards of truth for the purpose of getting along with others. Money and position seem to be their highest value. They appear

to love biblical principle, but only to the extent that it can earn them more money and more popularity among men. They flatter others while speaking evil of them behind their backs. Their Christianity is only skin deep and used only to impress people.

2. A benefice is a gift of land or a pastoral income. In the pre-Reformation years, a benefice was an income attached to an ecclesiastical office. Often priests would have access to multiple benefices and absent themselves from their parish(es) where they were supposed to serve. Mr. Money-Love's highest value is money. He constructs a complicated apologetic to defend a pastor's seeking a pulpit offering more money. He doesn't place any importance on any other spiritual value in the pastor's decision, nor does he mention the primary goal that should be in the mind of all Christians: "Seek the kingdom first, and all the material things will be added unto you" (Matt. 6:33).

3. Answers may vary. For this man, being religious seems to be a *means* to become rich and materially well-established.

4. Answers may vary. It would be hard to read Money-Love's heart motivation any differently based on his language. Truly, he wants to use Jesus as a "stalking horse" to obtain and enjoy the world (or money and power). Christian and Hopeful quickly leave these false brethren.

5. Demas, in the biblical record, was at one point a compatriot and brother of the Apostle Paul, but later he apostatized from the faith. In Paul's words, "Demas has forsaken me, having loved this present world." In this story, Demas tempts others to follow his apostasy. Promising filthy lucre (money), he lures these men into the pit where they die. This is not unlike Judas Iscariot and Gehazi (Elijah's servant), who strayed from the way for money. Also, the parable of the sower presents the seed sown in the thorns, where it is choked by the cares of this world (Matt. 13).

6. True Christians must abandon the values of the world—where men lust after pleasure, money, and power far more than the values of Christ and His kingdom. We must not look back with longing desire for the things of the world. Those who look back betray a heart condition that is not truly committed to the things of the Lord.

7. It looked more pleasant and far easier on the feet of weary pilgrims. It seemed to run parallel to the true Pilgrim pathway and thereby seemed appropriate for less-than-discerning Christian and Hopeful.

8. Pilgrims who veer from the pathway find themselves filled with doubt as they doubt God's existence, His salvation, and His presence as well as the purpose of their journey. Sometimes doubt leads to despair, and some pilgrims never make it out of the depths of this despair. Whether this refers to suicide or spiritual apostasy, it is hard to say. But this is a frightening, harrowing episode in the lives of these pilgrims in our story. Answers may vary. In the next book, Great-Heart and his brothers trash the castle and kill the Giant. It may be a more infrequent occurrence for some Christians in some church communities.

9. Hopeful reminds Christian of past history—how a faithful God gave them even more difficult trials and provided a way of escape. Hopeful keeps encouraging Christian to endure this trial with great patience, because God will most certainly deliver them from the hand of Giant Despair. They also pray together a great deal. The Sixth Commandment (the commands of God) prevents them from committing suicide.

10. They escape the castle by means of a Key called "Promise." The powerful promises of the Word of God, understood, realized, embraced, and applied to ourselves, work as a powerful tonic in the life of a Christian. Christian remembers that he has this Key called Promise. They escape the place just ahead of the Giant, whose limbs fail in the pursuit.

CHAPTER 8

Vocabulary
1. c
2. a
3. e
4. b
5. d

Questions
1. These are pastors in the Church of God, and they are shepherding.
2. They show the Pilgrims the Hill of Error where many men who have followed the teachings of heretics have fallen and been dashed to pieces. It is the duty of the pastors of churches to point out heresies that have taken many to destruction. The Shepherds also show these men the Hill Caution, from which they can see blind men stumbling about among the caves. They explain that Giant Despair gouged out their eyes and placed them among the tombs where they will eventually die. They also show them the pit that leads to hell, where they can hear the screams of those who suffer in everlasting torment. Again, it is the duty of pastors to issue the solemn warnings contained in Scripture concerning judgment and hell fire. Before parting, they warn of the Flatterer and the Enchanted Ground. The Christian life is indeed a dangerous journey, and the pastors are there to warn, guide, and encourage Christians along the way.

CHAPTER 9

Vocabulary
1. c
2. e
3. b
4. d
5. a

Questions
1. Little-Faith certainly struggled to make the journey.

He did not receive much comfort in his salvation along the way since it seems that he did not refer to his roll the entire way. Nevertheless, he kept faith through his trials and did not sell his heavenly treasures (the jewels). However, Turn-Away did turn completely away from the faith whereupon he was seized by devils and taken to hell. Some people who look promising on the outside at the beginning do not make it to the end while others, who appear to be struggling greatly the entire distance, will finally achieve the goal.

2. God places the strong with the weak that they might care for them. Great-Grace offers assistance to Little-Faith on the journey.
3. 3. It is the false teachers who make men feel good about themselves. Typically, their words are sugar-coated, and they refuse to lead God's people in the way of repentance. They do not face the people with hard lessons, nor do they shepherd them towards repentance. There is something sinister about this man in black, and yet his words are easily received by the fleshly sort. Paul refers to these deceitful teachers in 2 Corinthians 11:12-15: "And I will keep on doing what I am doing in order to cut the ground from under those who want an opportunity to be considered equal with us in the things they boast about. For such men are false apostles, deceitful workmen, masquerading as apostles of Christ. And no wonder, for Satan himself masquerades as an angel of light. It is not surprising, then, if his servants masquerade as servants of righteousness. Their end will be what their actions deserve."
4. They believe that the man is hopelessly lost in his deceit. They see no benefit in talking to him as it only breeds more arguing. They can tell that he will not be persuaded. Should one spend much time in debates with those who reject the truth of Scripture and the existence of God?
5. These are trusting in the treasures and riches of the world, rioting, reveling, drinking, swearing, lying, uncleanness (fornication), and Sabbath-breaking.
6. We are instructed in the Scriptures to remain watchful and sober, because our enemy the devil prowls about seeking whom he may devour. There are times in the Christian life when we become spiritually lethargic. We lose interest in the sermons, the reading of the Word, and prayer. If we do not struggle to stay awake and alert, these are times that could lead us out of the way and into serious sin.
7. Hopeful shared his testimony on how God worked in his life to bring him to where he is today.
8. It was Faithful's powerful testimony and martyrdom in Vanity Fair that led Hopeful to join Christian on this journey. Other powerful influences upon him included overhearing the reading of the Bible, witnessing the death of an acquaintance, and considering the possibility of his own death.
9. He is prideful and self-centered, trusting ultimately in himself rather than in God for his salvation.
10. Ignorance could not believe that the heart of the carnal man is depraved and not to be trusted. He wanted to trust his own heart and seemed not to rely upon the Word of God. He has really never seen his need for Christ because he has never seen the foul character of his own heart and his own sin. Also his view of justification is twisted as he thinks he will be accepted by God because of his own obedience (not Christ's obedience.)

CHAPTER 10

Vocabulary
1. d
2. c
3. a
4. e
5. b

Questions
1. Christian claims that ignorant men will stifle any true conviction of sin. The ignorant man is the foolish man who does not fear God.
2. Men are first temporarily awakened by a conviction of sin. But their fundamental mindset towards sin remains unchanged. Therefore, when their guilt wears away, they return to their former lifestyle as the dog returns to its vomit. They cease to consider any notions concerning God, death, and judgment altogether. Then, they cast off by degrees certain spiritual activities such as closet prayer, curbing lusts, sorrow for sin, and the like. After this, they begin to shun the company of lively Christians. Next, they will stop attending church or participating in any "godly conference." Then, they turn to gossip or slander against godly men. At this point, they will also take up company with evil men and engage in open sin. In short, they show themselves for who they really are. Answers may vary. Apostasy is biblically accurate (Matt. 13:1-20, Heb. 6:1-8). The process described here may vary for various apostates.
3. Death.
4. Heaven is described here as built with precious stones and pearls, with streets of pure gold. Reference Revelation 18:19-21.
5. Do not read too much into the dream. Don't be afraid to find fault with it. Study the principle of it rather than focusing on the superficial elements of the story. Take the gold and purge the dross.

BOOK TWO

THE AUTHORS WAY
1. Bunyan is interacting with Christiana, but it is as if she is still a character in a book or the book itself. It seems that he has given the story a personality.
2. It appears that others may have plagiarized his first book. He answers several objections to the first edition of the book in this little poem.
3. The book was enthusiastically received everywhere it went, including France and Flanders where severe

persecution continued for Christians.

TO THE READER

Vocabulary
1. b
2. a
3. d
4. e
5. c

Questions
1. She was saddened by the bond broken in the loss/death of her husband. God also impressed upon her soul the "unbecoming behavior," with which she had treated this husband who was now dead (gone over the river to the Celestial City). Recalling her husband's restless groans and heavy remorse for his sins further convicted her of her own sins. Finally, a messenger from the Celestial City arrived with a message from the King inviting her to embark upon the journey. The letter also included a promise of forgiveness which she began to take to heart. In the end, it was the dream she had and the messenger from the Celestial City that confirmed her desire to go to the City. One can see here multiple influences upon the lost soul that irresistibly draws her into the way.
2. There seems to be more detailed advice here for Christiana, whereas Christian was merely warned to "fly" from the impending destruction upon the City. It appears also that Christiana receives a letter at the beginning, which she is to deliver at the gate. Christian did not receive any "certificate" or "roll" until he came to the Cross. Also, we do not see a burden on Christiana's back although there is no question that she experiences the conviction of sin.

CHAPTER 1

Vocabulary
1. d
2. a
3. b
4. e
5. c

Questions
1. Mercy chose to go with Christiana because 1) she had a yearning to be with Christiana, and 2) her heart was concerned about her own spiritual state. Although it does not appear that she is entirely committed to the journey from the outset, she is willing to hear more about it as they go along the way. She says that if she finds truth and life in what Christiana shares with her, she will be willing to complete the journey with her.
2. They accuse her of willfully subjecting herself and her children to unnecessary dangers. Answers may vary. Many do think that Christians engage in unnecessary struggles and subject themselves to persecution when they could just issue a detente with the world.
3. False teachers in the Church have attempted to fill in the Slough of Despond with their own self-help books, etc.
4. This is an initial test of faith. God requires a seeking and a pursuing on the part of the enquirer, and throughout the Pilgrim journey, He tests our willingness to seek Him. The knocking at the gate is the initial test. Yes. It does appear that God will subject some to more severe tests of their faith. Some may knock for quite a while before they receive a response, others may tap once or twice. Moreover, by God's sovereign direction, the enemy sends his dogs and shoots his arrows at the enquirers standing there at the gate. These influences may be discouraging to some, but they encourage others to continue to knock with even more vehemence.

CHAPTER 2

Vocabulary
1. c
2. e
3. b
4. d
5. a

Questions
1. Sometimes the temptations of the world even make it into our godly homes and Church communities. It is interesting that many parents protect their children as much as possible from the "forbidden fruit" of the world, yet there are subtle ways in which these temptations worm their way into their homes and lives. The boys clearly disobeyed their mother in eating this fruit. Although the enjoyment of a "wicked" movie or hearkening to ungodly companions may be pleasant for a while—the end result is quite unpleasant as the story later reveals.
2. It appears that these men are intent to harm, rape, or kill the women. Yes. Some times and places are more dangerous than others. When women live alone (without a male protector), it seems that they may be more subject to the unfavorable advances of men like this. We ought not to be so naïve as to think that Christians are not subject to dangerous, harrowing circumstances. Bad things happen to "good" people. And Christians (especially men) ought to be well aware of their duties to protect their women and children. This is a dark element of the story. Undoubtedly, Bunyan is rendering a realistic picture of fallen, sinful men and the depths to which they will go to express their depravity.
3. There is sometimes a reticence at first to receive a Pilgrim. After a time of acquainting, things seem to warm up quickly as they discover that she is a true Pilgrim who desires to walk in the way. In this case a damsel named Innocence answers the door and asks Christiana's name. There is instant recognition of Christiana as the wife of Christian (the famed Pilgrim). Christiana confesses

her hard-heartedness. Innocence relates Christiana's case to the son (in Jesus' parable), who would not obey when his father instructs him to work in the vineyard but later repents and does the work. Obviously, it is a community that knows one another and knows who has and who has not taken the Pilgrim journey. What we see here is the joy we experience when our relatives, friends, and acquaintances embrace the truth. Sometimes, we pray with our brothers for 10, 15, or 20 years for the salvation of their spouses or other close relatives.

4. Some people will reject the Word when we share it with them, but later will take it to heart. It is like a seed that is dormant for a year or two, and then takes root and eventually brings forth fruit. On the other hand, there are some people who hear the Word, and seem to receive it with joy, but eventually they fizzle out.

5. About the only thing the average person cares about is making a living, keeping his beer supply well stocked, and what's on television tonight. He is almost like a cow who is constantly looking down at the earth for the next clump of grass it can eat. They cannot see anything of eternal value. They do not look forward to an eternal inheritance. Even if he attends Church from time to time, his general life philosophy is, "Eat, drink, and be merry, for tomorrow we die."

6. Answers may vary.

7. We wander astray like sheep (Is. 53:6). We are tended as sheep by Yahweh, our Shepherd (Psalm 23:1). The sheep know the voice of their Shepherd (John 10:13-16). We suffer tribulation and trials as sheep that are led to the slaughter (Rom. 8:32).

8. The fruit that God wants us to bear in our lives is the fruit of the Spirit, such as love, joy, peace, patience, kindness, goodness, gentleness, faithfulness, and self-control.

9. The robin is described as consuming the ugly spider when he is by himself. Ordinarily he makes a diet of crumbs. Many professing Christians maintain a facade when they are with other Christians. They appear to enjoy Christian fellowship and the worship of God. But when they are by themselves, their true heart manifests itself. They have a taste for sinful stories, television programs that encourage fornication, dishonor of parents, and other God-dishonoring behaviors. They enjoy ungodly fellowship when they are away from people of God. The true integrity of our hearts is made manifest when we are by ourselves and away from those who would hold us accountable to godly behavior.

10. Bunyan is referring to the sins of the flesh. A Christian can still sin and with Paul, cry out, "Oh wretched man that I am, who will deliver me from this body of death?" (Rom. 7). A field can produce good crops but still be coated with dung. A beautiful robin has been known to consume an ugly spider. The Interpreter is presenting pictures of the Christian life and providing means by which believers may understand their relationship with the world, the flesh, and the devil. He wants the pilgrims to be watchful and to pray, and to conform themselves to God's will in their lives.

11. Entertainment during the meals in Bunyan's day included both singing and dancing.

12. The bath is representative of Christian baptism, and the Passover Seal is more than likely their first Communion. It is interesting that in this latter segment of Pilgrim's Progress, Bunyan placed Baptism and the Passover Seal prior to the Cross.

CHAPTER 3

Vocabulary
1. b
2. a
3. e
4. c
5. d

Questions
1. Great-Heart is a valiant man, given the task of protecting and guiding pilgrims on their journey to the Celestial City. He is a pastor, a discipler, an elder, and a faithful guide. His particular charge was to get Christiana and her boys safely to the City and protect them from all the dangers which might befall them.

2. Christiana does not experience the same conversion experience that her husband experienced at the Cross. We do not see her burden rolling away, nor her receiving a new set of clothes or a roll. Nor do the three shining ones appear to her.

3. Extra Challenge: Many evangelicals today would put Baptism and the Lord's Supper after a single, definitive experience that could be labeled a "conversion experience." It seems that Bunyan does not emphasize a "conversion experience" in this second book, as he does with the first. Some believe that a single conversion experience is the primary mark of "becoming a Christian." But many Christians, especially those who were raised in the faith, cannot point out one particular time and place where they began to believe in Christ as Savior and Lord. Nevertheless, Bunyan rightly puts the Cross in the center of the Christian life, and Christ, in His person and work, as the object of our faith.

4. Pastor Great-Heart tells the pilgrims that pardon is an act of God for sinners. We are pardoned because Jesus Christ has imputed His righteousness to our account.

5. It is often in the midst of great difficulty that we become weary in the midst of the battle. We may temporarily rest during the battle, but that does not give us an excuse for a relaxation of vigilance—we must still be vigilant in case the enemy creeps upon us suddenly.

CHAPTER 4

Vocabulary
1. d
2. a

3. e
4. c
5. b

Questions
1. The bottle of spirits is distilled alcohol, and apparently was refreshing when taken in small doses.
2. Giant Grim is a fear monger. He is in the business of encouraging pilgrims to fear, whether it be fear of the future, fear of circumstances, fear of rejection, fear of persecution, or fear of devils and monsters. This giant just wants pilgrims to live in the grip of fear. Christians deal with their fear by looking to Jesus, singing, praying, and fellowshipping around the Word of God.
3. There seemed to be much discussion on a variety of issues. They prayed and sang psalms before retiring to bed. There isn't much in terms of television and man-oriented entertainment here.
4. Answers may vary. Bunyan may be replicating what is found in Acts when believers met "house to house." The line between small house meetings and public meetings (Acts 20:20) may be a little gray at points in the book of Acts as well as in *Pilgrim's Progress*. It does appear here that this is Christian Hospitality in a home.
5. She is catechizing the children. We find the question and answer form of catechizing in Exodus 13:14 and Deuteronomy 6:20. Catechisms appeared during the Reformation period. Luther's Catechism was one of the first written for children.
6. She was always finding things to do for others, like making clothes for the poor and needy.
7. Mr. Brisk is an interesting fellow who pretends to be religious, yet he seems to be more focused on succeeding in business than succeeding in the kingdom of God. Even in his support for the poor and needy, he seems more concerned with what people think about him than he does about caring for the poor.
8. The fruit of Beelzebub are the temptations that come, whereby men are drawn away by their own lusts and enticed (James 1:14). Typically these come by way of music, movies, advertisements, and books that tempt us to sin. Answers may vary. Websites, music, movies, etc.
9. Matthew was cured of the gripes by a combination of something called *ex carne et Sanguine Christi* and salt pills. He was to take these pills each day mixed with the tears of repentance. This Latin phrase is translated, "The body and blood of Christ." It is the clear teaching of the Word of God, conviction of sin, and the receiving of the body and blood of Christ for the forgiveness of sins that cures.

CHAPTER 5
Vocabulary
1. c
2. e
3. a
4. b
5. d

Questions
1. Great-Heart associates Christian's slipping down into the valley with the combat thereafter. One must traverse the valley carefully, and Christian might have been a little over-confident as he approached the valley. He also met this fierce foe because he was forgetful of what God had done for him previously. According to Mercy, one must sing, be of a contrite heart, and look unto Jesus and His work.
2. The psalms help us through this valley. One must continually cry out to God for light and deliverance. Samuel reminds us here that one must keep the end in mind as he trudges through this valley.
3. Giant Maul is a powerful giant who maintains very powerful systems of indoctrination whereby many simple people are led out of the way by false arguments, deceptions, and lies. This giant consumes the populace today by the millions. He spoils young people by sophistry, worldly wisdom, superficially plausible reasoning, and education systems that refuse to teach the beginning of wisdom as the fear of God. Entire entertainment systems, television networks, music production companies, universities and colleges, news wire services, etc. all present a worldview that counters a biblical approach to knowledge and life.

CHAPTER 6
Vocabulary
1. d
2. e
3. a
4. b
5. c

CHAPTER 7
Vocabulary
1. d
2. c
3. a
4. b
5. e

Questions
1. There are some places that are even darker than others where there is far less accessibility to the truth of the Word of God.
2. Mr. Fearing is fearful of anything that should offer the least resistance to him as he conducts his journey. He is a man of weak faith, yet he is still a man of faith. He is a humble man, constantly aware of his own unworthiness. God draws near to the humble and resists the proud (I Pet. 5:5, James 4:6). Mr. Fearing is far more dependent on God than on himself. Yet, he is fearful over whether he will be accepted in heaven at the end. Despite his weakness, he still relies upon God throughout the journey. And fundamentally, his fear of God is far more dominating in his life than fear of men or circumstances. He really did

not fear the lions before the House Beautiful.
3. The bass and sackbut are two of the most important instruments of an orchestra, providing the bass line for the music. It appears that Mr. Fearing preferred the doleful music of the bass and sackbut, yet what would life be like without them? Answers may vary.
4. The Fear of God is the beginning of all wisdom and knowledge. Fear is the foundation, the bass support of the rest of life. Without the fear of God, there can be no proper love for God or trust in God for salvation. If we fear God, we will not fear men or any other threat to our well-being.
5. He would use David's sin as an excuse for his own. If David and Solomon could sin in their adultery and polygamy, certainly he could avail himself of this sort of sin with impunity.
6. Parents seem to be involved here. They allowed the young people to get to know each other and made certain of their compatibility. Certainly, young people did not marry without parental consent.
7. He favored good discourse, intellectually stimulating riddles, theological discussion, edifying conversation, ministering to the poor, and good food and fellowship around the dinner table. The Christian life should include a great deal of hospitality, ministering to the poor, and a rigorous education that comes about around the dinner table. The family should also eat together and fellowship on a daily basis.
8. They are both of feeble constitutions and slower and weaker than the others in their faith. How do they differ from each other? Mr. Ready-to-Halt, although ready to halt, was of a more ready mind than Mr. Feeble-Mind. Mr. Feeble-Mind was very sickly and slower of mind, and did not have as cheerful a disposition.

CHAPTER 8

Vocabulary
1. d
2. a
3. b
4. e
5. c

Questions
1. Reference Acts 21:16. He was a man from Cyprus and one of the early disciples with whom the other disciples stayed while they were in Caesarea. Evidently, he is a man with some connection to Vanity Fair in this story, but he stays pure from the world. He provides protection, hospitality, and some degree of credibility for the pilgrims. Here Bunyan introduces a character into the story who is more *in* the world—less of a separatist and more of a puritan.
2. The world soon discovers that persecution usually only strengthens the Christian faith. But more than this, it takes a tremendous amount of concentrated energy to persecute good people, and also usually contributes to the breakdown of a civil state. Evidently, the blood of Faithful still weighed heavily upon the consciousness of this city, and there was something of the fear of God in the place. Answers may vary.
3. Answers may vary. The Bible makes several uses of the word "world." There is the world of trees, flowers, land, families, and civil governments. And then there is the world that we are to hate that is defined as "the lust of the flesh, the lust of the eyes, and the pride of life." It is the second world in which we are not to participate. It is quite appropriate for the Christian to be in the world of trees, flowers, families, and civil governments; yet we are not to embrace the world of lust and pride. Unfortunately, the world of lust and pride often dominates the world of flowers, land, art, and civil government. To the extent that we can sort it out, and avoid living a life of lust and pride, we may participate in this world's systems. This is the tension that John Bunyan is working with in this portrayal of Vanity Fair. You can see a more mature Bunyan grappling with these issues in his second book.
4. The dragon must represent Satan—that old dragon mentioned in Jeremiah and John's Revelation. Evidently, children are easily lured into the world where they are taught by the ungodly and are often nurtured by their peers who have taken on the attitudes, the clothing, and the culture of the world (through MTV, Hollywood, and other cultural systems). One puritan wrote that the first step towards Christian children leaving the faith is association with ungodly peers.
5. Jesus takes babies into His arms and blesses them in Mark 10:14, Luke 18:16, and Matthew 19:14.
6. Those who are alone are much more given to doubting, depression, and despair than those who are among a band of Christians who are filled with hope and joy. Strong, faith-filled leadership can have a wonderful influence upon hundreds of believers as they strip away doubt by faith-filled preaching of the Word of God!
7. Dancing was appropriate to celebrate victory or at some other special occasion requiring celebration. On witnessing God's astounding victory over the Egyptian army at the Red Sea, the women of Israel joined with Miriam for a victory dance. Also, David danced when the Ark returned to Jerusalem.
8. 1) The importance of prayer. We need faith in order to remove mountains, and faith to believe that our prayers will be answered. 2) The promise of God's preservation and hope. The righteous man, who has received the righteous garments of Christ, cannot be spotted by the world. Their righteousness will continue to break forth like the noon day. 3) The importance of caring for the poor. He who has a heart to give to the poor and exercise love/charity towards them will never lack himself.
9. It is the word of God that will never grow dull and is sharper than a two-edged sword. It is living and active and piercing to divide bone and marrow—incredibly powerful.
10. She is the Proverbs 7 woman, the temptress that takes many a man to hell with her. She tempts them to come and commit adultery with her, therefore taking them out

of the way and piercing them through with arrows. She tempts with her tongue, her facial expressions, her body positions, and her actions. Reference Proverbs 7.
11. She encourages others to strong faith, sobriety, watchfulness, and endurance to the end. She exhorts others to repent of their fear and doubt. All of this manifests a strengthening of faith over the years of her life.
12. The horses, the chariots, the trumpets, the singers, etc. signify a great celebration of rejoicing and glory for each saint who finishes the race.
13. In this glory that awaits us in heaven, we can see the importance of the valiant battle we wage on earth.

EXAM

Multiple Choice
1. C
2. D
3. A
4. C
5. B
6. A
7. B
8. D
9. B
10. D
11. B
12. C

Fill in the Blank
1. Christian enters the path through the *wicket* gate.
2. Christian flees to the Celestial City from the City of Destruction.
3. The name of Christian's two companions during his journey are *Faithful* and *Hopeful*.
4. In the second part, the protector of the Pilgrims is named *Great-Heart*.

Short Answer
1. Bunyan wrote *The Pilgrim's Progress* while he was in jail in Bedford.
2. Christian leaves behind his wife and children.
3. Giant Despair is killed and Doubting Castle is destroyed.

Essay Grading Criteria for _____

Student Essay Choice: #____

Directions: Grade the chosen essay based on the following four criteria, circling the number based on the student's apparent understanding of the subject and his or her ability to communicate these ideas in a clear and concise way:

1. Introduction clearly addresses essay topic

    Not at all   1 -----------2 -------------- 3 ------------ 4 ------------ 5   Absolutely

2. Grammar and sentence structure are well developed

    Not at all   1 -----------2 -------------- 3 ------------ 4 ------------ 5   Absolutely

3. Organization of essay shows development of the introduction

    Not at all   1 -----------2 -------------- 3 ------------ 4 ------------ 5   Absolutely

4. Conclusion helps summarize the substance of the essay topic within the word count

    Not at all   1 -----------2 -------------- 3 ------------ 4 ------------ 5   Absolutely

Grading: Each of the four sections is worth a total of 25 points, with a total of 100 points possible for the essay.

Note the total grade here: _____

Essay Grading Criteria for _____

Student Essay Choice: #____

Directions: Grade the chosen essay based on the following four criteria, circling the number based on the student's apparent understanding of the subject and his or her ability to communicate these ideas in a clear and concise way:

1. Introduction clearly addresses essay topic

    Not at all   1 -----------2 ------------- 3 ------------ 4 ------------ 5   Absolutely

2. Grammar and sentence structure are well developed

    Not at all   1 -----------2 ------------- 3 ------------ 4 ------------ 5   Absolutely

3. Organization of essay shows development of the introduction

    Not at all   1 -----------2 ------------- 3 ------------ 4 ------------ 5   Absolutely

4. Conclusion helps summarize the substance of the essay topic within the word count

    Not at all   1 -----------2 ------------- 3 ------------ 4 ------------ 5   Absolutely

Grading: Each of the four sections is worth a total of 25 points, with a total of 100 points possible for the essay.

Note the total grade here: _____

Essay Grading Criteria for _____

Student Essay Choice: #_____

Directions: Grade the chosen essay based on the following four criteria, circling the number based on the student's apparent understanding of the subject and his or her ability to communicate these ideas in a clear and concise way:

1. Introduction clearly addresses essay topic

    Not at all   1 -----------2 ------------- 3 ------------ 4 ------------ 5   Absolutely

2. Grammar and sentence structure are well developed

    Not at all   1 -----------2 ------------- 3 ------------ 4 ------------ 5   Absolutely

3. Organization of essay shows development of the introduction

    Not at all   1 -----------2 ------------- 3 ------------ 4 ------------ 5   Absolutely

4. Conclusion helps summarize the substance of the essay topic within the word count

    Not at all   1 -----------2 ------------- 3 ------------ 4 ------------ 5   Absolutely

Grading: Each of the four sections is worth a total of 25 points, with a total of 100 points possible for the essay.

Note the total grade here: _____

Essay Grading Criteria for _____

Student Essay Choice: #____

Directions: Grade the chosen essay based on the following four criteria, circling the number based on the student's apparent understanding of the subject and his or her ability to communicate these ideas in a clear and concise way:

1. Introduction clearly addresses essay topic

    Not at all   1 -----------2 -------------- 3 ------------ 4 ------------ 5   Absolutely

2. Grammar and sentence structure are well developed

    Not at all   1 -----------2 -------------- 3 ------------ 4 ------------ 5   Absolutely

3. Organization of essay shows development of the introduction

    Not at all   1 -----------2 -------------- 3 ------------ 4 ------------ 5   Absolutely

4. Conclusion helps summarize the substance of the essay topic within the word count

    Not at all   1 -----------2 -------------- 3 ------------ 4 ------------ 5   Absolutely

Grading: Each of the four sections is worth a total of 25 points, with a total of 100 points possible for the essay.

Note the total grade here: _____